The Bumper Irish
Jokebook

Published in 2007 by
Appletree Press Ltd
The Old Potato Station
14 Howard Street South
Belfast, BT7 1AP

Tel: +44 (0) 28 90 24 30 74
Fax: +44 (0) 28 90 24 67 56
E-mail: reception@appletree.ie
Web-site: www.appletree.ie

Design & Layout © Appletree Press Ltd, 2007
Text by Terry Adlam

A catalogue record for this book is available from the British Library.

The Bumper Irish Jokebook

ISBN: 978 1 84758 045 0

Desk & Marketing Editor: Jean Brown
Editor: Jim Black
Design: Stuart Wilkinson
Production Manager: Paul McAvoy

9 8 7 6 5 4 3 2 1

AP3384

The Bumper Irish
Jokebook

Terry Adlam

Appletree Press

Liam saw Shaun walking down the road carrying two house bricks.

'Where you going with the bricks?' asked Liam.

'I'm going round O'Malley's house,' answered Shaun.

'What for?' Liam questioned.

'Well last night, O'Malley put a brick through my window,' said Shaun. 'So I'm going round to do the same to his window.'

'Oh right,' said Liam. 'But why two bricks?'

'Because,' replied Shaun, 'O'Malley's got double glazing.'

✳ ✳ ✳ ● ✳ ✳ ✳ ● ✳ ✳ ✳

Mary and Colleen met in a wine bar, ordered a drink and sat down at a nearby table.

'So,' asked Mary, 'how's your husband?'

'Compared to what?' replied Colleen.

✳ ✳ ✳ ● ✳

An Irishman was told by his landlord that he had two days to pay his overdue rent, otherwise he was out.

'Fine,' said the Irishman. 'Can I have Easter Sunday and Christmas Day?'

Liam and Shaun were mountain climbing, when Liam suddenly fell into a 400 feet deep crevasse.

'Liam, you alright?' shouted Shaun.

'I'm alive!' called Liam.

'Great,' called a relieved Shaun, 'I'll throw you a rope. Grab it and I'll pull you up.'

'I can't grab it,' shouted up Liam. 'I've broken both my arms.'

'Fit it around your legs, then,' instructed Shaun.

'Can't do that either,' said Shaun. 'I've broken my legs as well!'

'Well put the rope in your mouth,' Shaun called.
So Liam put the rope in his mouth and Shaun began to pull him up. Liam was almost at the top of the crevasse when Shaun called out.

'Are you alright Liam?'

Liam said, 'Yea..h..hhhhhhhhhhhhhhhhhhhh!'

~~~~~~~~~~~~~~~~~~~~~~~~~

Liam found Shaun painting a window frame so furiously that he was making a mess of it.

'Shaun, take it easy,' said Liam. 'Why are you working so fast?'

'I'm trying to finish this window frame before the paint runs out,' replied Shaun.

An Irishman is backing his car into his garage, when he runs over his cat, Rover, and kills it stone dead. Next to the ex-cat is a lamp. The Irishman picks up the lamp and rubs it, and sure enough a genie appears. Not a very big one, more of a teenie genie. Anyway the genie grants him one wish.

'Bring Rover back to life, please,' asks the Irishman.

'I'm so sorry,' says the teenie genie. 'That wish is just too difficult to grant.'

'OK, what about her?' says the Irishman, pointing to his wife who is sitting in the car.

'What about her?' questions the teenie genie.

'Make my wife beautiful.'

The teenie genie takes a look at the Irishman's wife then says, 'Hang about, let me have another look at that cat.'

~~~~~~~~~~~~~~~~~~~~~~~~~~~~~~~

They had a comedy night in the local pub and an Irishman wasn't impressed because of all the Irish jokes being told. By the time of the last act he had had enough.

'Oy,' shouted the Irishman. 'Stop the Irish jokes. You're making us all out to be a bunch of stupid eejits. In fact, if you tell another Irish joke, I'm coming up there and I'm gonna knock yer block off.'

Obviously taken aback the ventriloquist started to apologise. 'I'm very sorry...'

'You keep out of it!' shouted the Irishman. 'I'm talking to the little fella on yer knee.'

Mary went to the local police station to report that her husband was missing.

'OK,' said the desk sergeant, not looking up. 'Let's have a few details. What was he like?'

'Well,' began Mary, 'he was 27 years old, 6ft 2", he had long dark wavy hair and he was absolutely drop dead gorgeous.'

'I see,' replied the desk sergeant, looking up from his note and instantly recognising Mary. 'Wait a minute, you're Mary. I know your husband. He is fat, short, balding and over 50 years old.'

Mary looked crestfallen. 'I know,' she said, 'but sure who'd want him back?'

❋ ❋ ❋ • ❋ ❋ ❋ • ❋ ❋ ❋

Finnegan had died and as he lay at rest at home, friends and family came to pay their last respects.

'It's so sad,' said one friend to his grieving widow, 'and yet he looks so happy.'

'I know,' said the wife, 'Finnegan always was slow on the uptake.'

❋ ❋ ❋ • ❋ ❋ ❋ • ❋ ❋ ❋

'What do you have in that bag?' asked Liam when he met his mate Shaun.

'Chickens,' said Shaun.

'If I guess how many there are in the bag,' said Liam, 'can I have one?'

'If you guess how many there are in the bag, you can have both of them.'

A couple were visiting a small Irish village and admiring its traditional setting and ways. The wife approached a strange-looking yokel leaning up against a gate.

'Excuse me,' she said politely. 'This village is so rural and well, so traditional, I was wondering if you still have a village idiot?'
The yokel looked at her and shook his head.

'Ah now Missus, I'm afraid we don't have a single village idiot at all at all.'

'Oh,' said the wife, disappointed.

'No,' continued the yokel, 'we all take it in turns.'

❋ ✳ ❋ • ❋ ✳ ❋ • ❋ ✳ ❋

Building site foreman, Ivor C. Mentmixer, was very worried when his top Irish brickie, told him that if he didn't give him a rise he would have to leave, owing to the fact that he had three other companies after him. Ivor was less worried when he found out that the companies were the Gas Board, the Electricity Board and the Water Board.

❋ ✳ ❋ • ❋

SPORTS NEWS!
The inaugural Irish Jockey steeplechase was finally abandoned this afternoon because the horses couldn't get a decent grip on the church roof.

It was the Dublin Winter Olympics and the Bulgarian skater Onmebum Mostofdatime raced on the ice rink and promptly fell over. Ever the professional, the skater got to his feet and continued his routine in a disastrous way, falling over more times than he stood up.

At the end of the routine he received no points from any of the judges, apart from the Irish judge who gave him 8.5 points.

When the Irish judge was asked by a confused official why he had scored the skater so high, he replied, 'Well, he did well. Sure it's ever so slippery out there.'

~~~~~~~~~~~~~~~~~~~~~~~~~~~~~~~~~~~

A young Irish boy comes racing home to his mammy very excited.

'Mammy, Mammy,' he squealed. 'You'll never believe it, but I was walking past the baker's and guess what I saw?'

'What did you see?' asked his old mammy.

'I only saw that they had made cakes with my signature on them.'

Old mammy was curious. 'Did they now. And did you buy one?'

'I did better than that Mammy, I bought two. Look!' He opened the bag he was carrying and his old mammy looked in.

'Oh yes, that's very nice darling. Some people call them Hot Cross Buns.'

Famous theatrical agent, Arthur Noon-Matinee was walking past a Galway building site when he saw Paddy perform a double somersault off some scaffolding, a back flip off a pile of bricks, a cartwheel over a cement mixer and execute a perfect landing. Arthur went rushing up to the Site Manager, introduced himself and said that he must book Paddy for a forthcoming show.

'You'll have to book Thaddy as well,' said the Site Manager.

'Why is that?' asked Arthur.

'Because,' said the Site Manager, 'Thaddy was the one who hit Paddy's thumb with the sledgehammer.'

An Irishman was in a shopping centre when he saw a sign: 'Dogs must be carried up the escalator'.
He spent the next two hours looking for a dog!

An Irishman walked into his local barbers and asked how much a haircut was.

'Five pounds,' said the barber.

The Irishman thought for a while and then asked, 'How much for a shave?'

'That's only a pound,' replied the barber.

'OK then,' said the Irishman, 'shave me head.'

Dermot O'Toole was an actor from Dublin of limited range and had been out of work, or as he called it "Resting, Darling," for quite a long time.

Then one day his agent rang to say he had got him a part in a play with a Belfast Theatre Company. The part only had one line, but it could be the break that O'Toole was looking for.

O'Toole took the job and began rehearsing straight away. The line was 'Hark, is that a cannon I hear?'

He rehearsed the line on the way to the station in the taxi: 'Hark, is that a cannon I hear?' He repeated the line over and over again on the journey to Belfast and in the cab to the theatre: 'Hark, is that a cannon I hear?'

He was still repeating it when he was shown to his dressing room and as he got into his costume.

'Hark, is that a cannon I hear?'

'Hark, is that a cannon I hear?'

There was a knock on his door. 'Five minutes Mr O'Toole!' called the Stage Manager.

'Hark, is that a cannon I hear?' O'Toole continued calmly.

A while later there was another knock. 'One minute, Mr O'Toole.' O'Toole rehearsed and rehearsed: 'Hark, is that a cannon I hear?'

'Hark, is that a cannon I hear?' he repeated over and over as he walked from his dressing room to the stage and one more time in the wings just before he was about to go on stage.

Then his moment came. O'Toole strode on to the stage and there was a blinding flash and an enormous bang.

'Oh Bejasus!' he shouted. 'What the divil was that?'

An Irishman saw a man on a bridge about to jump off, so he rushed up to him.

'Don't jump man! Think of your wife and children.'

'I've haven't got a wife or children,' said the man.

'Well, think about your parents?'

'I'm an orphan.'

'Well then, think of St Patrick.'

'Who's St Patrick?' asked the man.

That was when the Irishman pushed him.

✳ ✳ ✳ • ✳ ✳ ✳ • ✳ ✳ ✳

Paddy was visiting Pat in hospital. Pat had broken nearly every bone in his body and was covered, apart from his mouth, from head to toe in plaster.

'Blimey Pat,' said Paddy, 'your parachute jump didn't go that well, did it?'

'No,' groaned Pat.

'What happened?' asked Paddy.

'Me parachute didn't open,' Pat mumbled.

'Oh dear!' commiserated Paddy.

'You should have got an Irish parachute. Y'know, the ones that open on impact.'

Mr and Mrs O'Rourke were on holiday in Spain and they kept hearing the expression 'Manyana.' So they asked their guide Juan Phorderoad what it meant.

"Mañana',' began Juan, 'translates as, "Maybe the job will be done soon, maybe tomorrow, maybe the next day, maybe the day after that. Perhaps even next week, or month or year, who cares?" 'Mañana'.'

'Well now, that's very interesting!' said Mrs O'Rourke.

Juan smiled. 'Tell me, do you have a similar expression in Ireland?'

'No,' said Mr O'Rourke, 'we rarely have that degree of urgency.'

Now, no one is saying that O'Malley was tight with money, but he did get rid of his barometer when he found out his wife had flu.

When her temperature reached 110 degrees Fahrenheit, he put her in the cellar to heat the house up!

Did you hear the one about the Irishman who tried to repair a gas leak in his local hospital?

Doctors informed his wife that he was on a life support machine, a bed, the curtains, the ceiling, the windows...

An Irishman was sent out by his wife to get some edible snails for a dinner party they were having that evening, Off he went and bought about a dozen, then on the way home he popped into his local for a quick one, or two, or three or...

Well, come closing time, he had had more than enough and had missed the dinner party. On his wobbly way home he knew he was in big trouble. Sure enough when he got home he looked through the letterbox and there was his wife waiting for him, and she wasn't looking too happy.

So the Irishman put the snails on the doorstep and opened the door saying loudly:

'Now come on lads, hurry up, otherwise I'm in big trouble.'

A group of young Irish boys had formed their own ten-piece Rhythm and Blues band and were playing their first gig. The lead singer was very excited by the event and asked one of the sax players to go outside and listen to what they sounded like.

Sure enough the saxophonist went outside and after while came running back, very excited.

'You should hear it!' he said excitedly. 'It sounds brilliant!'

So the whole band went out to listen...

A holidaymaker was making his way to the bathroom in Mary's bed and breakfast.

'Excuse me, Sir,' Mary said. 'Do you have a good memory for faces?'

The holidaymaker stopped at the bathroom door and said, 'Yes I do actually.'

'That's great,' said Mary, 'because there's no mirror in the bathroom.'

✳ ✳ ✳ • ✳ ✳ ✳ • ✳ ✳ ✳

Shaun met Liam and asked, 'Have you seen O'Riley lately?'

'A good question,' said Liam, 'because I have and I haven't.'

Shaun was confused (well wouldn't you be?).

'What do you mean by that?'

'Well, I was walking down the road the other day,' began Liam, 'and I saw someone who I thought was O'Riley, and he said that he thought he saw someone he thought was me. But when we got up close... it was neither of us.'

✳ ✳ ✳ • ✳ ✳ ✳ • ✳ ✳ ✳

Mary and Colleen were enjoying another glass of wine and a chat in another winebar:

'For his birthday, my husband wants to go somewhere he's never been to and do something he's never done before,' said Mary.

'So where are you sending him?' asked Colleen.

'To the kitchen to do the ironing!' said Mary.

An Irishman came home looking very upset.

'What's up?' asked his wife.

'I've been sacked from me job on the one-man bus,' he said.

'Why?' his wife questioned.

'Because the bus crashed and they said it was my fault.'

'What happened?'

'I don't know,' replied the Irishman. 'I was upstairs collecting fares at the time.'

✻ ✻ ✻ ● ✻ ✻ ✻ ● ✻ ✻ ✻

Moylan noticed that Doylan was looking very sad as they met in the street.

'What's the matter?' asked a concerned Moylan.

'I've lost me dog,' moaned Doylan, 'and I can't find him.'

Moylan said, 'Why don't you put an advert in the local paper?'

Doylan stared at Moylan in bewilderment.

'Don't be daft. You know he can't read.'

Liam was watching Shaun dig a hole in his garden.

'Shaun,' called Liam 'where are you going to put all that soil when you've dug that hole?'

'I'm going to dig another hole and put it all in that,' Shaun smugly replied.

'Ya eejit,' laughed Liam. 'Then you'll have all the soil from that hole left over.'

'No I won't,' answered Shaun even more smugly than the last time, 'because I'm going to dig that hole much deeper.'

~~~~~~~~~~~~~~~~~~~~~~~~

Two Irishmen were playing snooker together for the first time. They had been playing for nearly two hours without potting a single ball and thoroughly enjoying themselves when one of them whispered:

'Do you think we should take that wooden triangle off the balls?'

~~~~~~~~~~~~~~~~~~~~~~~~

A little Irish girl had lost her mammy in a busy supermarket and was crying.

'What's the matter?' asked a friendly shop assistant.

'I've lost me mammy!' bawled the little Irish girl.

'Now, now, don't worry,' said the friendly shopkeeper. 'We'll find her. Now tell me, what's she like?'

The little Irish girl stopped sobbing, and said, 'Bingo, 'Coronation Street', Tom Jones, Dad going away on business...'

'So,' said Arthur Noon-Matinee, the well-known theatrical agent, to an Irishman. 'You do bird impressions.'

'That's right, Sir,' replied the Irishman.

'And what do you do exactly?' Sir Arthur asked. 'Nightingale, Skylark, Chaffinch?'

'No Sir,' said the Irishman. 'I eat worms.'

A man burst into the bank brandishing a firearm and screamed at the teller behind the counter.

'Hand over all the money. Do it quick and no one will get hurt.'

'You're Irish, aren't you?' enquired the unperturbed bank clerk.

'Yes!' said the Irishman. 'How did you know?'

'You've sawn off the wrong end of your shotgun,' came the calm reply.

An Irishman was sitting in the park enjoying some fish and chips when a woman with a small dog sat next to him. The dog could smell the fish and chips and got quite excited and kept jumping up at the Irishman and yelping.

'Excuse me, Miss,' said the Irishman. 'Do you mind if I throw your dog a bit?'

'Not at all,' smiled the woman.

So the Irishman picked up the dog and threw it into the duck pond.

A man went into an Irish optician to complain about his failing eyesight so the Irish optician took him outside and pointed up into the sky. 'What can you see up there?' he asked. The man looked up and replied, 'the sun.' The Irish optician said, 'Well, how far do you want to see?'

Freddy O'Flipper trained hard to become the first Irishman to swim the Irish Sea and the day came when he was ready. Things started off well and Freddy swam hard and strong. Halfway across the sea he was tired but still determined. This determination carried him onwards, but unfortunately with the shore just in view Freddy was exhausted. There was just no way he was going to make it. Disappointed, he turned around and swam home.

Tom walked into Mick Kanic's garage and said, 'Mick, I've got a problem with my car.'

'What is it?' asked Mick.

'It's a form of transport powered by an internal combustion engine,' answered Tom.

'No,' sighed Mick, 'I meant, what's the matter with your car?'

'Oh, there's water in the carburettor,' replied Tom.

'We'll soon get that sorted out,' smiled Mick confidently. 'Where's your car?'

'The fire brigade are just fishing it out of the river as we speak,' said Tom.

A little Irish girl was in class learning the alphabet, when her teacher asked her:

'So, what comes after 'T'?'

'The Six O'clock News!' the little Irish girl replied.

✳ ✳ ✳ • ✳ ✳ ✳ • ✳ ✳ ✳

Two Irishmen had decided to take up duck hunting, so off they went on their first shoot. Eight hours passed and not one duck had they bagged.

'This duck hunting isn't as good as it's made out to be,' said one of them. 'We've been here all day and what have we got? Nothing. That's what!'

'I know,' agreed the other one. 'Do you think we're not throwing the dog high enough?'

✳ ✳ ✳ • ✳ ✳ ✳ • ✳ ✳ ✳

Sweethearts Geri and Terry were sitting on a park bench bathed in the romantic sheen of moonlight.

'If I won the Lotto,' began Geri, 'I'd get myself a new house and a new swimming pool and a new car and a new motorbike and a new boat, and a new wardrobe of clothes, and...'

'Darling,' Terry softly interrupted, 'what about me?'

'...a new boyfriend,' continued Geri.

An Irishman rang up the 'Guinness Book of Records' to tell them that he had just completed a 1000 piece jigsaw in three weeks. 'It must be a world record!' he said excitedly.

'Why do you think that?' asked the man from the 'Guinness Book of Records'.

'Because on the box it says "two to five years".'

'This is a very unusual chair,' the Irishman said to his dentist. 'Most dentist's chairs go up and down, don't they? This one just goes backwards and forwards. It's quite unusual.'

Then the dentist said, 'Mr O'Malley, please get out of the filing cabinet.'

An Irishman was at his Mammy's house and noticed a number of empty milk and beer bottles in his fridge.

'Mammy,' asked the Irishman, 'why are there empty milk bottles in the fridge?'

'Ah,' said his Mammy, 'that's just in case anyone comes round and wants a black coffee.'

'What about the empty beer bottles?' the Irishman asked again.

'They're for people who come round who don't drink.'

An Irishman hobbled out of a Dublin hospital on crutches, with both his legs in plaster. He met his friend, who was going into the hospital for the results of his dope test, and his friend stopped him.

'Hey!' he said. 'What happened to you?'

'I've broken both my ankles,' said the Irishman. 'That's the last time I try to make my own coconut wine.'

Have you heard the one about the new Irish video recorder?

It records the programmes you don't want to see, and shows them when you're out!

It was announced on television recently that Delia O'Burnt-it the famous Irish TV chef had got fed up making chocolate chip cookies.

Apparently it took her too long to peel the Smarties.

Did you hear the one about the Irish schoolboy who was a bit on the thick side?

When he was at school he always used to play truant two days a week. Then he found out that the other kids didn't go to school on Saturdays and Sundays either!

An Irishman got a job on the dustcarts. It was a job he picked up quite quickly. In fact he was so good, that he could carry a bin under each arm and balance another one on his head.

One day his friend saw the Irishman carrying all his bins and whistling happily.

'Wow,' said his friend. 'That's fantastic. How do you do it?'

'It's easy,' grinned the Irishman. 'I just puts me lips together and blow.'

An Irish couple were on holiday in Melbourne, Australia and they were visiting the grave of Captain Cook.

'I wonder how he died?' asked the wife.
The husband thumbed through the guidebook and found the appropriate page. 'It says here that he was murdered.'

'I'm not surprised,' replied his spouse, 'especially after what he did to Peter Pan and Wendy!'

Liam looked up from his *Book of Interesting Facts* and turned to Shaun. 'It says here that a camel can go for five hundred miles without water.'

'That's amazing,' gasped Shaun, 'can you imagine how far he could go with water!'

Did you hear the one about the Irish boy who arrived home one day carrying a settee under one arm and an armchair under the other?

His mammy told him off for taking suites from strangers!

❋ ✳ ❋ • ❋ ✳ ❋ • ❋ ✳ ❋

An Irish girl went to see her doctor, Dr R.U. Inpain with a very badly burnt ear.

'How on earth did that happen?' enquires the doctor.

'Well,' says the Irish girl, 'I was doing the ironing when I heard the phone ring…'

❋ ✳ ❋ • ❋ ✳ ❋ • ❋ ✳ ❋

An Irishman went up to the counter in a shop.

'I'd like *Shrek 2* please.'

'I'm sorry, Sir,' said the shopkeeper, 'but this is a fish and chip shop.'

'Oh?' said Irishman. 'I'll have *A Fish Called Wanda*, then.'

❋ ✳ ❋ • ❋

'So children,' smiled the teacher. 'Can you name six animals that come from Africa?'

'Sure can, Miss,' beamed the confident little Patrick. 'An elephant, a lion and four giraffes.'

A young Irish boy was watching his father whittle away at a piece of wood in his workshop.

'What you making, Daddy?' asked the little Irish boy.

'A portable,' replied his father.

'A portable what?' asked the little Irish boy again.

'I don't know yet,' said the Irishman. 'I've only just made the handle.'

An Irishman went into a men's clothes shop and spoke to the assistant behind the counter.

'Excuse me, but I'd like to return this tie and get my money back.'

'No problem, Sir,' said the Assistant. 'Didn't you like the colour?'

'No,' replied the Irishman. 'It was too tight.'

An Irishman went into his local fish shop 'In Cod We Trust' late one night, and asked the owner if he could borrow twenty pounds.

'I'm afraid you can't,' said the owner, 'on account of the arrangement I have with the bank.'

'What arrangement?' asked the Irishman.

'They don't sell fish and chips and I don't lend money,' replied the owner.

Paddy saw Thaddy digging a hole in his garden.

'What're you doing?' asked Paddy, noticing that the garden was already covered with a number of other holes.

'My dog died,' said Thaddy, wiping his brow, 'so I'm digging a hole to bury him in.'

'So what are those other holes for?' enquired Paddy.

'They were other holes I'd dug to bury the dog in,' replied Thaddy, 'but they weren't big enough.'

Did you hear the one about the Irishman who enrolled at night class?

He thought they would teach you to read in the dark!

A white horse trots into a Dublin pub and orders a drink.

'Hey!' says the barman. 'We've got a whiskey named after you.'

'What, Dobbin?' said the horse.

Mary and Colleen were enjoying yet another glass of wine and a chat in another local wine bar.

'I read somewhere,' said Colleen, 'that bigamy is when you are married to one man too many.'

Mary sighed. 'I would say that monogamy is very much the same.'

An Irish landlord was very concerned when the brewery told him that they couldn't deliver any stout to his bar.

He knew that if he didn't do something he would lose customers and money. So he came up with a brilliant idea. He gave all his regulars sunglasses and served them lager!

❋ ❋ ❋ • ❋ ❋ ❋ • ❋ ❋ ❋

An Irishman went into a pizza restaurant and ordered a pizza with all the trimmings. When it was ready the cook asked, 'Do you want me to cut it into four or eight slices?'

The Irishman thought for a while and then said, 'Best cut it into four slices – I'll never be able to eat eight.'

❋ ❋ ❋ • ❋ ❋ ❋ • ❋ ❋ ❋

Did you hear the one about the Irishman who was caught illegally importing cheap Irish workers into Ireland?
He was found guilty of dope smuggling!

❋ ❋ ❋ • ❋ ❋ ❋ • ❋ ❋ ❋

Mary and Colleen were enjoying a glass of wine and a chat in their local wine bar 'The Grapes of Waterford.'

'My husband says that if there is such thing as reincarnation, he wouldn't mind coming back as a pig,' said Mary.

'What did you say to that?' asked Colleen between sips.

'I told him that wouldn't happen, because you have to come back as something different.'

Having done the football pools for many, many years, an Irishman was very excited when a man from Littlewoods finally knocked on his front door.

'Does this mean I've won the Pools?' asked the very excited Irishman.

'No,' replied the man from Littlewoods. 'We've just caught your wife shoplifting.'

✳ ✳ ✳ • ✳ ✳ ✳ • ✳ ✳ ✳

An Irishman was in his local butchers and fishmongers, 'Whale Meat Again', when a great big Alsatian bounded in and snapped up a couple of pounds of sausages from the counter and ran off.

'Hey!' shouted the butcher to the Irishman. 'Wasn't that your dog?'

'He was,' replied the Irishman calmly, 'but he fends for himself these days.'

✳ ✳ ✳ • ✳ ✳ ✳ • ✳ ✳ ✳

An Irishman sold his friend a donkey, but two weeks later his friend was on the phone.

'That donkey you sold me?'

'What about it?'

'It's just dropped dead.'

'Has it?' replied the surprised Irishman. 'It never did that when I had it.'

A young Irishman brought three girls home to meet his Mammy.

'Mammy, I'm getting married to one of these lovely girls. Can you tell which one?'

'The one in the middle!' she said straight away. The young Irishman was shocked.

'Mammy, that's amazing. How did you know?'

'I don't like her,' snarled his Mammy.

'Well, how did you get on?' asked an Irishman's wife when he returned home from a job interview with a well-known German car manufacturer.

'I didn't get the job,' sighed the Irishman.

'Why not?' said the Irishman's wife.

'I couldn't spell BMW.'

An Irishman rang his wife up in a very excited state.

'Get packing... I won the Lotto!' he screamed.

His wife was obviously delighted.

'Wow, that's great news. I'll start right away. What shall I pack? My summer clothes for a tropical holiday or my skiwear or something glamorous?'

'Pack what you like,' said the Irishman. 'Just make sure you are out of the house when I get home.'

Two Irishmen were in an art gallery looking at some statues.

'See that statue over there?' said one. 'It's 1000 years and 12 weeks old.'
His friend was impressed.

'Wow, that's amazing! How did you know that is the exact date?'

'Because,' he replied, 'when I came here 12 weeks ago, one of the guides told me it was 1000 years old.'

Did you hear about the Irish water polo team?
All their horses drowned!

'Do you know the difference between a Dublin wedding and a Dublin funeral?' an Irishman asked.

'No, I don't,' replied his friend.

'One less drunk.'

An Irishman is up at the bar in a Belfast pub and says, 'Hey, I've got some great Paddy Scotsman jokes.'
The barman's such a big fella he makes Desperate Dan look like a nine stone weakling.

'Look, before you start, I'm warning you, I'm Scottish.'

'Oh, no problem,' says the Irishman. 'I'll tell them very slowly.'

An American in need of a toilet was hurrying through a dockyard when he stopped O'Malley, an Irish docker, man and boy.

'Howdy partner,' the Yank drawled, 'do you know where the urinal is?'

O'Malley looked around and then said, 'No idea Sir. How many funnels does it have?'

❋ ❋ ❋ • ❋ ❋ ❋ • ❋ ❋ ❋

'And so,' announced Seymore Starrs, head of the Irish space programme proudly to the assembled Press. 'We have finally built Ireland's first manned rocket, *The Begorah 1*.'

'And when will it be launched?' asked an eager journalist.

'As soon as we find a big enough bottle,' replied Seymore.

❋ ❋ ❋ • ❋ ❋ ❋ • ❋ ❋ ❋

NEWSFLASH!

A special police squad were called in to a resolve a tricky situation yesterday. Unfortunately things didn't go to plan when the leader misheard his orders.

He led a dawn raid on Dublin Zoo and successfully released 25 ostriches.

Two Irishmen were at an air display and were marvelling at the aerobatics the planes were performing.

'You know what?' said one. 'I wouldn't like to be up there in one of those things.'

'You know what?' replied his friend. 'I wouldn't like to be up there without one!'

❋ ❋ ❋ • ❋ ❋ ❋ • ❋ ❋ ❋

'I was really close to winning the Lotto last week!' Liam said to Shaun.

'Really?' asked Shaun. 'How many numbers were you out?'

'Six,' said Liam.

❋ ❋ ❋ • ❋ ❋ ❋ • ❋ ❋ ❋

Two Irishmen wanted to check that the indicators on their car were working. One of them went round the back to check.

'Yes they are, no they're not, yes they are, no they're not...' he called.

❋ ❋ ❋ • ❋

MEDICAL NEWS!
The Irish have just set up a new clinic for people who want to stop smoking. It's called Smokers Anonymous.

Any time you get the urge to light up a cigarette, you just ring them up and they send a man over and you get drunk together instead.

Sam Which the Irish baker decided that he was going to save money by making bigger holes in his doughnuts. It didn't work, because he found that the bigger he made the hole the more dough he needed to go around it.

'Mammy, can I have an ice cream?' asked a little Irish girl.

'No!' said her mum. 'It's too cold.'

The little Irish girl thought for a while and then said, 'Mammy, can I have an ice cream if I put my coat on?'

O'Shalley met O'Malley in the street and asked him why he was wearing a neck brace and had his arm in a sling.

'Oh, I had an accident when I was raking up some leaves,' groaned O'Malley.

'What happened?' asked O'Shalley.

'I fell out of the tree.'

'I'm afraid your pet chameleon is dead,' said Dr Downboy, the vet, to the Irishman. 'It appears to have died from exhaustion.'

The Irishman sighed. 'I knew I should have never put its cage next to those disco lights.'

An Irishwoman went to her solicitors Grabit, Haveit and Run, and said that she wanted a divorce from her husband.

'I see,' said Will Grabit. 'Do you have a grudge?'

'No,' said the Irishwoman. 'We only have a carport.'

An Irishman went into a café and asked if the owner would fill his flask up with coffee.

'Of course I can,' said the café owner. 'Give it to me.'

'Thank you,' smiled the Irishman, handing over the flask. 'I'll have six cups; two black, three white and one without sugar please.'

Did you hear the one about the Irish seasickness tablets?

They really work – you just take one with a glass of water and then you are seasick!

An Irishman went into a café and asked if the owner would fill his flask up with coffee.

'Can you lend me a tenner?' Thaddy asked.

'Of course I can,' said Paddy, 'as soon as I get paid.'

'When will that be?' Thaddy enquired.

'As soon as I start working,' replied Paddy.

An American tourist walks into an old country pub in Tipperary.

'Hey man, what a quaint ol' Irish pub,' he says. 'It's got a real atmosphere and look, it's even got sawdust on the floor.'

The barman looks at him.

'That's not sawdust, that's last night's furniture.'

❋ ✳ ❋ • ❋ ✳ ❋ • ❋ ✳ ❋

An Irishman was in the optician's picking up his new glasses.

'Right,' said the optician Dr Seymore Clearly, 'here's your new glasses. Now your eyesight isn't too bad, but you must wear them when you're working.'

'Oh,' said the Irishman, 'that might be a problem.'

'Why's that?' asked the optician.

'I'm a boxer,' replied the Irishman.

❋ ✳ ❋ • ❋ ✳ ❋ • ❋ ✳ ❋

A little Irish girl was at the lounge table doing her geography homework while her Dad was watching the football on the television.

'Dad!' she called. 'Where are the Himalayas?'

Without looking away from the TV her dad said, 'I don't know. Ask your Mum, she puts most of the stuff away in this house.'

A little Irish girl came home from school looking very pleased with herself.

'Mammy, I won a prize today in nature studies.'

'That's nice,' said Mammy. 'How did you win?'

'Well, the teacher asked the class how many legs an emu has, and I said four.'

'Four?' questioned Mammy. 'But an emu has two legs.'

'I was the nearest,' smiled the little girl.

✳ ✳ ✳ • ✳ ✳ ✳ • ✳ ✳ ✳

An Irish farmer was trying to raise chickens, but it just wasn't working.

'I just don't know what I'm doing wrong,' he said to his wife.

'Perhaps you're planting them too deep?' she replied.

✳ ✳ ✳ • ✳ ✳ ✳ • ✳ ✳ ✳

The manager of a Dublin football team was giving a pep talk before the start of a big cup match.

'OK boys, we're in trouble today because everything in our favour is against us.

'The referee has just told me that it's getting foggy out there, so he might be playing extra time first. So what I think is this, we've got to equalise before they score to have a chance of winning the game.'

A cook had just started working in an Indian restaurant in Dublin when he collapsed and the Manager had to call the paramedics.

'What happened?' asked the Irish paramedic.

'Well,' said the Manager, 'he was making a meal and sampling some of the ingredients, when he just passed out.'

'Which ingredients was he sampling?'

'Um, well... a bit of cumin, some turmeric and a couple of other spices,' replied the Manager.

The Irish paramedic sighed. 'Well, that explains it then.'

'Why, what's wrong with him?' demanded the Manager.

'He's in a korma,' he said.

~~~~~~~~~~~~~~~~~~~~~~~~~~~~

It was very cold and an Irishman decided to go fishing. He started to dig a hole in the ice when he heard a big booming voice call:

'Do not cut a hole in the ice.'

The Irishman looked around but couldn't see anybody, so he finished the hole and started to fish in the ice. Then came the big booming voice again.

'Do not fish in the ice.'

The Irishman was confused. He couldn't see anybody, but he thought for a while, and then he said aloud:

'Is that you God talking to me?'

'No,' said the booming voice. 'It's the Manager of the ice rink.'

Did you hear the one about the Irish restaurant that said they served a 7-course Irish meal?
They gave you a potato and a six-pack of stout!

'What ya doing pardner?' called the American tourist when he saw an Irishman digging in his garden.

'I'm digging up me potatoes,' said the Irishman picking up a potato to show the American.

'Call that tiny thing a potato?!' drawled the American. 'Back home we have potatoes ten times the size of that.'

'Ah yes Sir,' said the Irishman, 'but we only grow ours to fit our mouths.'

Paddy Englishman, Paddy Scotsman and Paddy Irishman had escaped from prison and were in a barn hiding in some sacks when the police came.

A policeman kicked the sack Paddy Englishman was in and Paddy Englishman went, 'Miaow.'

'Just a cat in that sack,' said the policeman. Then he kicked the second sack and Paddy Scotsman went, 'Quack, quack.'

'Just a duck in that one,' said the policeman.
It was going so well. Then the police kicked the last sack and Paddy Irishman went, 'Potatoes.'

'Has that Irish girl been using the computer to write letters again?' asked an angry Boss.

'Yes she has,' said one of her work colleagues.

'I thought so,' sighed the Boss. 'There's Tippex all over the screen again.'

An Irishman went into a pet shop and bought 99 budgerigars, tied them to himself, jumped off a cliff and plummeted to the ground. The next day he limped back to the pet shop, bought 99 chickens, tied them to a kite, took a painful running jump off the same cliff, and once again plummeted to the ground. The following day he returned to the pet shop on crutches and covered in bandages. He asked for 99 parrots.

'I hope you don't mind me asking?' said the pet shop owner. 'You've had 99 budgies and 99 chickens, why do you want 99 parrots?'

'Well,' said the Irishman. 'That budgie-jumping and hen-gliding were a waste of time so I thought I'd have a go at parrot-chuting.'

Did you hear the one about the Irish burglar?
He broke into a bookie's and lost twenty pounds!

Mary and Colleen were finally coming home from the winebar and were staggering along.

'Colleen,' asked Mary looking up into the sky, 'is that the sun or the moon?'

'I don't know,' replied Colleen. 'I don't live around here.'

Liam asked Shaun if he could borrow a file.

'What for?' Shaun asked.

'Well, my hamster has got a bit of hard skin on the top of its head and I want to file it off.'

'You can't do that,' said Shaun. 'You'll kill it!'

'No I won't,' replied Liam. 'I'll be gentle.'

So Shaun gave Liam the file.

A couple of days later Liam returned the file.

'How did it go?' asked Shaun.

'Oh the hamster died.'

'I told you it would,' Shaun boasted. 'I told you not to use a file.'

'Oh it wasn't the file that killed him,' said Liam. 'I think I had him in the vice too tight.'

✳ ✳ ✳ • ✳ ✳ ✳ • ✳ ✳ ✳

Did you hear about the Irish girl who asked her mammy for an encyclopaedia for Christmas?

Her mammy said 'No' and that she could walk to school like the rest of the kids.

✳ ✳ ✳ • ✳

'Hey this e-bay is good,' said Pat. 'I've just sold my television for fifty pounds.'

'That's great,' said Paddy. 'What are you going to do with the money?'

'Well I've got enough money to buy a video recorder now.'

An Englishman, a Scotsman and an Irishman go into a bar and they all order a Guinness. Suddenly a fly drops into the Englishman's drink.

The Englishman sees the fly, stares at it for a few moments, then picks it up and throws it in the Scotsman's glass.

The Scotsman sees the fly in the head of his Guinness, stares at it for a few seconds, shrugs his shoulders and drinks the beer. He spits the fly into the Irishman's pint.

The Irishman sees the fly and quickly grabs it and starts to shake it saying, 'Spit it out! Spit it out!'

~~~~~~~~~~~~~~~~~~~~~~~~~~~~~~

It was Molly Malone's first day working at the restaurant and the manager called her over.

'Molly, why has it taken you four hours to fill up four salt-cellars?'

'I'm sorry,' apologised Molly, 'but it's very difficult to get the salt into that little hole in the top of the lid.'

~~~~~~~~~~~~~~~~~~~~~~~~~~~~~~

Did you hear the one about the Irishman who decided to enter the Dublin marathon?

He started to train very hard. For six weeks he ran 5 miles a day. The training was going well but at the end of the six weeks he was 210 miles away from the race!

An Irish girl went to her physician, Dr Ann Nurses, to complain about a strange pain she was experiencing.

'Doctor,' she said, 'every time I drink a cup of tea I get a sharp stabbing pain in my eye.'

'That sounds unusual,' replied the Doctor. 'Why don't you make a cup of tea now, so I can see what happens.'

So the Irish girl made a cup of tea and sure enough she got the sharp stabbing pain in her eye.

'Ah, I see the problem,' smiled the Doctor.

'What is it?' asked the Irish girl, concerned.

'Well, when you make another cup of tea, remember to take the spoon out before you drink it.'

Two Irish workmen were working on a building site.

'The boss says we're getting a thousand bricks delivered today,' said one.

'A thousand?' replied his friend. 'How many is that?'

'Oh millions…'

A man saw a sign in an Irish restaurant window that read, 'CHICKEN DINNER 50p'. Thinking this a bargain, he went in and ordered a chicken dinner for 50p. A few minutes later the Irish waiter returned and set down a plate of grain.

'What's this?' asked the surprised man.

'It's grain, Sir,' said the waiter.

'But I ordered a chicken dinner!' the man protested.

'Well,' sniffed the Irish waiter, 'it's what our chickens get for dinner.'

An Irish girl stood by the roadside while the vehicle breakdown man looked under the bonnet of her car.

'Ah, that's your problem,' he said after a few minutes of investigation. 'You've got a flat battery.'

'Oh,' said the Irish girl. 'What shape is it supposed to be?'

Two Irishmen had been stranded on a desert island for over three years when one day a boat washed up on to the beach.

'Quick, quick!' shouted one of the Irishmen excitedly. 'Look what I've found.'
His friend came running over and was delighted.

'At last!' he cried. 'We can leave the island and return home.'
So that night the two friends set about chopping up the boat to make a raft.

A man saw a sign at an Irish restaurant that read, 'ALL MEALS AT VERY POPULAR PRICES' so he went in and ordered soup.

When he finished his meal, the Irish restaurant manager gave him the bill and the man was shocked.

'£10 for a bowl of soup!' he exclaimed. 'I thought all your meals were at popular prices?'

'Well, I like them,' said the manager.

An Irishman went on *Mastermind* and after 'Passing' when the Quiz-master asked him his name, he was given another question.

'How many 'D's are there in *Indiana Jones and The Last Crusade*?'
The Irishman thought for a while and then said '110.'

'110!' laughed the Quiz-master. 'How on earth did you work that out?'

'Easy,' said the Irishman as he counted on his fingers. 'De De De, Dee, Dah, Dah Daaa, De, De, De, Dee, Dah, De, Dah Dah Daah! De, De, De....'

✳ ✳ ✳ • ✳ ✳ ✳ • ✳ ✳ ✳

Have you heard the one about the Irishman who sits out in the garden when it is sunny?

Just the merest hint of sunshine and he stops what he was doing and goes outside to relax in amongst the flowers and grass.

He's called Paddy O'Furniture!

✳ ✳ ✳ • ✳

Did you hear about the Irishwoman who wanted an animal skin coat for her birthday?
Her husband bought her a donkey jacket!

Two Irishmen were discussing their forthcoming holiday.

'So where are you going?' asked the first Irishman.

'America,' said the second.

'Oh, where?'

'Hippopotamus,' replied the second Irishman.

'Where?'

'Hippopotamus,' replied the second Irishman. 'It's near Niagara Falls.'

'You mean Buffalo,' sighed the first Irishman.

'I knew it was some sort of big animal.'

It's been announced recently that the gallant attempt to be the first All-Irish team to climb Mount Everest has failed. The courageous team led by Irish Mountaineering expert, Cliff Face, tried very hard and would have made it to the summit, but they ran out of scaffolding.

An Irishman was up in court and as he stood in the dock, the Judge, who had no thumbs and was known as Justice Fingers, gave him a hard stare.

'Tell me, is this the first time that you've ever been up before me?'

The Irishman was confused and stared back at the Judge.

'I don't know your honour, what time do you generally get up?'

There was a power cut in the Delaney household just as the doctor was about to deliver Mrs Delaney's baby.

'What shall I do Doctor?' asked nervous Mr Delaney.

The doctor told Delaney to go and get a lantern and hold it up so that the doctor could see what he was doing, which is what Mr Delaney did.

Soon the baby arrived. Mr Delaney was about to put the lantern down when the doctor said, 'wait a minute, hold the lantern up.'

Mr Delaney did as he was told and a few minutes later there was another baby. Then there was another and another.

'Doctor,' asked Mr Delaney, 'do you think it's the light that's attracting them?'

'So how's the new diet going?' Shaun asked Liam when they met in the street.

'Oh it's brilliant,' replied Liam. 'It's a whiskey diet.'

'A whiskey diet?' said Shaun in surprised tones.

'Yeah, I have whiskey for breakfast, whiskey for lunch, whiskey for dinner and whiskey for supper.'

Shaun was impressed and asked, 'is it working?'

'Well I lost three days last week,' said Liam.

An old dishevelled three-legged Irish wolfhound limps into a saloon in the Old Wild West. He limps across the floor and drags himself up to the bar. The bartender looks at this sorry creature and asks what he wants.

The old dog replies in a husky voice, 'I'm looking for the man who shot my paw.'

✳ ✳ ✳ • ✳ ✳ ✳ • ✳ ✳ ✳

A man went in to an Irish newsagent and asked for a newspaper.

'Would you like today's or tomorrow's?' asked the newsagent.

'Erm, I'll have tomorrow's,' said the man.

'OK,' said the Irish newsagent. 'Come back in the morning.'

✳ ✳ ✳ • ✳ ✳ ✳ • ✳ ✳ ✳

An Irishwoman was stopped by the police and was asked if she could show them her driving licence.

'I wish you people would make your minds up,' said the angry Irishwoman.

'Yesterday you took away my licence and today you want me to show it to you!'

✳ ✳ ✳ • ✳ ✳ ✳ • ✳ ✳ ✳

Did you hear the one about the Irishman who was very unhappy, even though he sold his house at a very good price?
His landlord sued him!

An Irishman is out for a stroll along the riverbank when he sees his friend, on the opposite bank.

'Hey!' he shouts. 'How can I get to the other side?' His friend looks up and down the river and shouts back.

'Ah, don't worry about that, you're already on the other side."

※ ＊ ※ ● ※ ＊ ※ ● ※ ＊ ※

'Is that Belfast double three, double three?' asked the voice when an Irishman answered the phone.

'No,' said the Irishman. 'This is Belfast 3333.'

'Oh, I'm so sorry to have bothered you,' said the voice.

'Not to worry,' said the Irishman. 'The phone was ringing anyway.'

※ ＊ ※ ● ※ ＊ ※ ● ※ ＊ ※

An Irishman rang the maternity ward and said excitedly, 'I'm going to bring my wife in. She's going to have a baby.'

'Is this her first baby?' asked the nurse on the other end of the line.

'No!' said the Irishman. 'It's her husband.'

'I only boil my eggs for two minutes,' Colleen told Nolleen when she popped round for breakfast.

'Why only two minutes?' asked Nolleen.

'Well if I held them in any longer, the water would burn my hand.'

A weary hiker was walking past a farm in Galway when the farmer asked him if he would like to come in for something to eat. The hiker was very hungry and took the farmer up on his offer. Sitting in the farm kitchen enjoying a large bowl of soup, he was amused to see a pig scurrying around and sniffing at his legs.

'Your pig is a curious little chap,' said the hiker.

'Not really,' said the farmer. 'He's just hungry, and he's waiting for you to finish with his bowl.'

Two Irish builders were flying over the Sahara Desert. One of them looked out of the plane's window.

'Will you look at all that sand?'

'Aye,' replied his friend. 'I wonder when the cement is going to be delivered?'

Liam was looking very shocked when he came round to Shaun's house.

'What's the matter?' asked a concerned Shaun.

'I woke up this morning and an aeroplane crashed into the side of my house.'

'That's awful!' Shaun gasped. 'What happened?'

'It's OK, no one was hurt but I must have left the landing light on.'

Farmer O'Malley kept two horses and had great difficulty telling them apart.

He tried putting them in separate fields, but that didn't work. He tried giving them different names, but that didn't work. Finally he came up with a solution.

He measured them both and found out that the black one was bigger than the white one.

Two Irish farmers were leaning on a gate looking at a herd of cows in a field.

'I bet I can tell you how many cows there are in that field before you,' said the first farmer.

'You're on,' said the second farmer, and started counting.

He hadn't got far when the first farmer said, '100.'

'Wow,' said the second farmer, 'how did you do that so quickly?'

'Easy, really,' said the first farmer. 'I just counted all the legs and divided by four.'

An Irishman went on *Stars In Their Eyes* and when Cat Deeley asked him who he was going to be? the Irishman said,

'Tonight Cat, I'm going to be Glenn Miller.'

The studio audience applauded as the Irishman disappeared into the smoke... and was never seen again.

✳ ✳ ✳ • ✳ ✳ ✳ • ✳ ✳ ✳

'My missus is never satisfied,' moaned an Irishman to his friend.

'Why's that?' asked the friend.

'Well, it was her birthday and I asked what she wanted and she said something with diamonds in it. So I got her something.'

'And didn't she like it?' said the friend.

'Nope!' sighed the Irishman. 'She threw the whole pack of playing cards back in my face.'

✳ ✳ ✳ • ✳ ✳ ✳ • ✳ ✳ ✳

Brendan was standing in the hallway 'suited and booted' ready to go out, but his wife was still getting ready.

'Bridget!' he called. 'Will you hurry up woman, otherwise we'll be late and miss the film.'

'Oh hold yer whist, Brendan McDougall!' shouted back his wife. 'Haven't I been telling you for the last hour, that I'll be ready in a couple of minutes?'

A Welsh mum, a Scottish mum and an Irish mum were chatting while they were waiting for their children to come out of school.

'I called my little boy, David,' said the Welsh mum, 'because he was born on St David's Day.'

'Oh that's nice,' said the Scottish mum. 'In fact I called my little boy Andrew, because he was born on St Andrew's Day.'

'Well isn't that strange.' said the Irish mum. 'I did the same. Oh, here he comes now.' She waved at her little boy and said, 'Hello Pancake, how was school today?'

✳ ✳ ✳ • ✳ ✳ ✳ • ✳ ✳ ✳

The foreman on the building site was surprised to see his Irish builder hopping along a plank of wood that stretched across two pieces of scaffolding.

'Oi,' called the foreman, 'why are you hopping?'

'I don't think this plank will take my full weight.'

✳ ✳ ✳ • ✳

Did you hear about the Irish swimming baths?
They had to close lanes 3, 4 and 7 due to hot weather and a water shortage!

A police officer stops two Irish drunks as they stagger out of the pub.

'OK lads,' says the policeman, 'what are your names and addresses?'

The first drunk says, 'My name is Michael Mulligan of no fixed address.'

'I see. And what about you?' the policeman asks the second drunk.

'Oh, I'm Dolan Dougan and I live in the flat above Michael.'

It was an Irishman's first day working at the sawmill when the manager saw him leaping about and clutching his hand.

'What's the matter?' he asked as he rushed over to help.

'I've lost me finger!' screamed the Irishman.

'How did you do that?' said the manager.

'Well,' said the Irishman, 'I just touched this big spinning thing here like thi... Ahh! There goes another one!'

Did you hear about the Irish Uri Geller?

He could bend spoons, forks, knives, anything, completely in half just by rubbing them. Unfortunately the other day he had a neckache and tried to rub it better, but his head fell off!

An Irishman was driving home one night and had stopped at some traffic lights when a policeman on a bike pulled up beside him and tapped on the window.

'At last!' said the policeman breathlessly.

'I've been after you since that last roundabout.'

'What is it officer?' asked the Irishman.

'Did you know that your wife fell out of the car when you went round that roundabout?'

'Oh thank goodness for that,' sighed the Irishman. 'For a minute there, I thought I'd gone deaf.'

'Hello,' said the man who knocked on Mr O'Grady's door. 'I'm collecting for the local swimming baths.'

'Oh right,' said Mr O'Grady. 'Wait here.'

Off Mr O'Grady went into the house and came back a couple of minutes later with a bucket of water.

An Irishman was having terrible trouble running up and down a tall ladder with a tape measure.

'What're you doing?' asked his friend.

'The boss wants me to measure this ladder.'

'Well, why don't you lay it down and measure it?' suggested the friend.

'That'll be no good,' said the Irishman. 'He wants the height, not the length.'

An Irishman rang up his local newspaper and asked how much it would be to put a 'For Sale' advert in the paper.

'That's a pound an inch,' replied the person from the paper.

'Oh that's far too expensive,' said the Irishman. 'I've got a 12ft ladder to sell.'

The head of the Irish Football Playing Association called a press conference to make an important announcement.

'Ladies and Gentlemen,' he began, 'I've called you all here today to announce that we have picked the team to represent Ireland in the next World Cup. It's Brazil.'

Did you hear the one about the Irishman who ran into his local DIY shop and covered himself in white, green and blue paint?

He was arrested and eventually taken to hospital, where the doctor said that he was suffering from emulsional distress!

An Irishman's neighbour caught him letting his dog foul the path right outside his gate.

'Oy!' shouted the angry neighbour. 'Why don't you train your dog to do that in the gutter?'

'I did,' said the Irishman, 'but he kept falling off the roof.'

An Irishman was walking down Dundalk High Street minding his own business when a man stopped him and asked, 'Excuse me, do you know if there is a B&Q in Dundalk?'

The Irishman thought for a while, and then a bit longer, and finally said, 'No, but there are two Ds and a K.'

❋ ❋ ❋ • ❋ ❋ ❋ • ❋ ❋ ❋

An Irishwoman wasn't that keen on having cable television, on account of the workman having to dig all those trenches. Her husband finally persuaded her to have it, by telling her that they could always get a new carpet when the workman had gone.

❋ ❋ ❋ • ❋ ❋ ❋ • ❋ ❋ ❋

'This is Aer Lingus flight 5673 to Control.'

'Come in Aer Lingus 5673, this is Control.'

'Control, we are flying at an altitude of 21,000 feet. One of my stewards has reported a faulty fuselage door and is at this moment holding on to it.'

'OK, Aer Lingus 5673, can you ask the steward to just let go of it for a second and see how far it moves?'

'Will do, Control.'

'This is Control to Aer Lingus flight 5673. Has the steward let go of the door?'

'Yes he has, Control.'

'And how far did it move?'

'About 21,000 feet, Control.'

A man was walking past a farm in Galway when he saw a farmer in a field with a three-legged pig.

'You don't see too many of those,' called the man.

'That pig, Sir,' said the farmer, 'is a hero. 'That pig woke me and my family up when the farmhouse caught alight last week and that pig led us to safety. When the fire brigade got lost, that pig, Sir, found them and led them here. And that pig then went back into the flames and rescued the cat, just getting out before the top floor fell through.'

'Is that how he lost his leg?' asked the man.

'Oh no Sir. When you've got a pig that is that brave and heroic, it seems a shame to eat him all at once.'

~~~~~~~~~~~~~~~~~~~~

An Irish girl was working behind the counter at the Post Office when a man came in with a letter and asked for a first class stamp.

The Irish girl gave the man the stamp and he asked, 'Do I put this on myself?'

'No ya big eejit,' said the Irish girl. 'Sure you stick it on the envelope.'

~~~~~~~~~~~~~~~~~~~~

'I thought you were supposed to come round and fix my doorbell yesterday,' moaned the irate woman when O'Hara the handyman arrived on her doorstep.

'I did. I rang twice, but got no answer.'

Aer Lingus flight 2347 was just coming into Shannon Airport when the Controller called on the radio.

'Aer Lingus flight 2347, you have traffic at 3 o'clock, 7 miles out.'

'Could you help us out on that?' asked the pilot. 'We're all wearing digital watches.'

Two Irish hunters were looking at some tracks on the ground.

'I reckon those are deer tracks,' said the first Irishman.

'No, I think they are fox tracks,' replied his friend.

'Deer!' argued the first Irishman.

'Fox!' argued the other one back.

They were still arguing when the train ran them over.

An Irishman went up to the woman behind the counter and said in a loud voice, 'I'd like a pint of the black stuff and a packet of cheese and onion crisps, please.'

'Sir, this is a library!' said the woman, quietly.

'Oh sorry,' apologised the Irishman. Then he whispered, 'I'd like a pint of the black stuff and a packet of cheese and onion crisps, please.'

Boylan and Moylan were staggering home from the pub along a country road as black as the pints they had been drinking. Suddenly Boylan tripped over something.

'Are you OK, Boylan?' called Moylan.

'I'm fine,' slurred Boylan. 'But I think we're in a graveyard.'

'Why do you say that?' asked Moylan.

'Because I can see a stone here that says a man lived to 110!'

Moylan was amazed. '110! Was it anybody we knew?'

'I don't think so,' Boylan burped. 'He was Miles from Galway.'

Liam found Shaun standing in front of his old garden shed looking very confused.

'What's wrong Shaun?' asked Liam.

'Oh I want to whitewash my garden shed,' replied Shaun, 'but I'm not sure what colour I want to do it in.'

There was an Irish restaurant that claimed it could serve any meal requested, so a man went in and asked a waiter for an Elephant and Tortoise sandwich.

The Irish waiter looked very embarrassed.

'Aha, you can't give me that can you?' said the smug man. 'I've caught you out haven't I?'

'You certainly have Sir,' said the Irish waiter. 'We've completely run out of bread.'

An Irishman went into his local barber shop and playground equipment suppliers called 'Short Back and Slides'. He asked the barber:

'Excuse me, I wonder if you can help me. My hair keeps falling out. Do you have anything for that?'

'Certainly Sir,' said the barber, giving the Irishman a paper bag. 'Here, keep it in this.'

❋ ❋ ❋ • ❋ ❋ ❋ • ❋ ❋ ❋

An Irishwoman had a rare medical condition, but made an amazing recovery after an operation that involved replacing some of her brain cells with cells from pig's skin. The operation was a success, but there was an unusual side effect. Her hearing was no longer the best, especially her left ear. She got a lot of crackling in it.

❋ ❋ ❋ • ❋ ❋ ❋ • ❋ ❋ ❋

An Irishwoman runs into a police station.

'Help me!' she screams. 'I just seen a man get in my car and steal it.'

'OK madam, calm down,' says the Desk Sergeant. 'Could you possibly describe the man?'

'No,' says the Irishwoman. 'But I did get the car registration number.'

Two Irishmen were playing 'Trivial Pursuit'. One of them rolled the dice and it landed on Science & Nature.

'OK,' said his friend, 'here's your question. If you are in a vacuum and someone calls your name, will you be able to hear it?'

The Irishman thought for a while and then asked, 'is it on or off?'

'They're a couple of fine looking animals,' commented a man when he saw an Irishman taking his dogs for a walk.

'Thanks,' said the Irishman. 'The black one is called Rolex and the brown one is called Timex.'

'Unusual names for dogs,' the man said.

'Not really,' said the Irishman, 'they are watch dogs.'

Paddy went round to Thaddy's and saw him in the living room just staring at a pile of wooden doors, shelves, brackets and screws.

'What's up, Thaddy?' asked Paddy.

'Oh it's this self-assembly furniture I've just bought. It's rubbish,' moaned Thaddy. 'I've been watching it for three hours now and it still hasn't done a thing. If I have to wait any longer, I'm going to do it myself.'

An Irishman was doing 90mph down a motorway when the police stopped him. The Irishman said he was going so fast because he had diarrhoea and he wanted to get home before it was too late.

The police let him off, but warned him it was a very dangerous thing to do, even more dangerous if he had been driving a car at the time.

An Irishman was about to get on a bus with his pet monkey.

'Hey!' said the conductor. 'You can't bring that thing on my bus.'

'Why not?' asked the Irishman.

'I'm talking to the monkey.'

Another Irishman was about to get on a bus with his pet crocodile.

'Hey,' said the conductor, 'you can't bring a crocodile on my bus. What're you doing with it? You should take it to the zoo.'

'I did!' said the Irishman, 'and today I'm taking him to the cinema.'

Dylan the village drunk, when to his doctor, Dr D. Kat. After a thorough examination the doctor said, 'I've had a good look at you. I know it's the drink, but I can't really say what is wrong with you.'

'Sure, that's all right, Doc,' said Dylan. 'Shall I come back when you're sober?'

An Irishman was looking very pleased with himself.

'So why are you looking so pleased with yourself?' asked his friend.

'Well,' said the Irishman, 'I made my wife's eyes light up last night.'

'Really?' replied his friend. 'What did you do? Buy her a present? Take her out for a meal?'

'Nope,' smiled the Irishman. 'I shone a torch up her nose.'

❋ ＊ ❋ • ❋ ＊ ❋ • ❋ ＊ ❋

An Irishman was showing his friend his new smart business cards.

'Very nice,' said his friend.

'Thanks.'

'Just one thing,' his friend added. 'Why have you had your named printed on the front and the back of the card?'

'Ah that's in case,' said the Irishman, 'I give one to someone and they lose it.'

❋ ＊ ❋ • ❋ ＊ ❋ • ❋ ＊ ❋

The Limerick Hotspurs Rover's goalkeeper let in 28 goals in one match. He trudged off the field feeling so dejected and with a nasty backache from all that bending over and picking the ball out of the back of the net. He slunk into the changing room, where all his team mates completely ignored him. He was so upset and distraught that he put his head in his hands to cry... and missed.

An Irishman was just about to leave the house, when his wife noticed he was only wearing one glove.

'Darling,' she called, 'why are you only wearing one glove?'

'Because,' the Irishman replied, 'the weather man on the telly said that it might be cold today, but on the other hand it could be warm.'

＊ ＊ ＊ • ＊ ＊ ＊ • ＊ ＊ ＊

An Irishman was telling his Mammy about the time he went to see *Titanic* at the cinema.

'It was a great film,' said the Irishman, 'but I had to stay in the cinema for ages after the film ended.'

'Why was that?' asked his Mammy.

'They were only letting women and children out first.'

＊ ＊ ＊ • ＊ ＊ ＊ • ＊ ＊ ＊

'Doctor, I'm worried about my wife,' the Irishman said. 'She's convinced that she's a bird.'

'That is very worrying,' said the Doctor. 'Tell you what, bring her in and I'll have a look at her.'

'I can't do that,' replied the Irishman.

'Why not?' asked the Doctor.

'She's just flown south for the winter.'

A judge rings up an Irish lawyer.

'How much would you charge me to answer three questions?'

'£1000, your honour,' replied the Irish lawyer.

'£1000!' exclaims the judge. 'That's very expensive, isn't it?'

'To be sure it is your honour,' answered the lawyer. 'And what's your last question?'

An Irishwoman went to see her doctor.

'It's my son, doctor,' she said. 'He keeps making mud pies and eating them.'

'There's nothing to worry about,' said the doctor. 'He'll grow out of it.'

'I hope so, Doctor,' said the Irishwoman, 'because his wife is getting very upset about it!'

Did you hear about Ireland's worst shepherd?
He used to call his sheepdog by putting his fingers in his mouth and shouting 'Rover!'

How did Ireland's worst shepherd count his flock?
'One sheep, Two sheep, Three sheep, another one, another one and another one and...'

An Irishman went into his bank for an appointment with his Bank Manager. He was invited into the Manager's office and got straight to the point.

'I was wondering Sir, how do I stand for a £500,000 bank loan?'

The Manager looked at the Irishman and said, 'On your knees.'

Sir Dinsmore Kildare, that famous Irish theatre actor was looking for lodgings in Belfast where he was about to appear in a play. He went up to one B&B, knocked on the door. The landlady appeared.

'Ah my good woman, I am seeking some accommodation in this fine city, whilst I perform for the lovely people within. This abode does indeed seem the ideal venue for one to rest before, and after, giving ones self in the name of ones art. Tell me pretty maiden, do you perchance have any low terms for actors such as I.'

'Certainly!' said the landlady. 'Clear off you pompous old eejit. Will that do?'

It was Christmas Eve in one particular Irish household and the husband was arguing with his wife.

'It's the same every year!' he bellowed. 'You're never satisfied. I buy the turkey, I pluck the turkey and I stuff the turkey. All you've got to do, woman, is kill it!'

An Irishman pulls up at a garage in his vintage car and fills it up with petrol. While he's paying the cashier says, 'that's an old car you got there.'

'You're telling me,' says the Irishman. 'It's the only car I know that's insured against fire, theft and Viking raids.'

'Wow!' says the cashier.

'That's nothing,' says the Irishman. 'I took the radiator out and found the original fireplace behind it.'

* * * • * * * • * * *

An Irishman was stuck in a traffic jam at some road works and he saw a sign for the Cone Hotline. He got on his mobile and rang them.

'Is that the Cone Hotline?'

'Yes it is,' said the lady on the other end.

'How can I help you?'

'I'd like a '99 with crushed nuts and raspberry sauce please,' said the Irishman.

* * * • * * * • * * *

An Irish couple were having an argument and the husband said,

'Do you know, I was a complete eejit, when I married you?'

'That's right,' replied his wife, 'but I was in love at the time and didn't notice!'

Nola O'Nolan takes her car into a local garage to have some dents removed. The mechanic knows to look at her that she isn't the brightest woman in Ireland, and it's nearly 5:30 on a Friday afternoon.

'You don't need me to take those dents out. Just take the car home and then blow up the exhaust pipe and the metal will pop back into place.'

Nola thanks the mechanic and takes the car home. Nolan O'Nolan, her husband, hears a huffing and puffing sound from behind the car. He opens the kitchen window and shouts,

'Nola, what on earth are you doing?'
Nola tells him what the mechanic had told her to do.

'You stupid woman,' says Nolan. 'It won't work with the windows down!'

❋ ❋ ❋ • ❋ ❋ ❋ • ❋ ❋ ❋

A visitor was walking past an Irish farm when he saw the farmer lifting a pig up to an apple tree and holding it while it ate the apples off the branch.

'Excuse me,' said the visitor. 'If you just shook the tree so that apples fell to the ground, wouldn't it save time?'

'Doesn't matter, really,' said the Irish farmer. 'The pig's got plenty of time.'

A tourist was driving through the Irish countryside when his car broke down. When he was looking under the bonnet to see what was wrong, he heard a voice say, 'Your clutch is gone.'

The tourist looked around and all he could see was an old horse in a nearby field standing at a gate. The horse looked at him and said in a thick Irish accent, 'I'm telling ya, it's the clutch.'

The tourist nearly died with fright, and ran into the nearest pub and ordered a large drink and told the barman what the horse had said to him.

'Oh don't take no notice of him,' said the barman, 'he knows nothing about cars.'

A spy was dropped into an Irish village with instructions to meet up with a contact by the name of Flynn. He was told that the recognition code to use was, 'It looks like rain.'

The first man he met was a farmer – he asked where he could find Mr Flynn.

'Now, Sir,' said the farmer, 'which Mr Flynn would that be, as we have a number of Flynns in this village? We have Father Flynn, Dr Flynn, Judge Flynn, Flynn the Undertaker, Flynn the Postman, Flynn the Chemist, Flynn the Mechanic, Flynn the Vet… In fact I'm a Flynn too. I'm Farmer Flynn.'

The spy had an idea and said, 'it looks like rain.'

'Ah,' smiled the farmer, 'you'll be wanting Flynn the Spy.'

Moylan was fishing by the river when Boylan came up to him.

'Caught anything yet?'

'Nothing,' replied a disappointed Moylan.

'What are you using for bait?' asked Boylan.

Moylan lifted his line out of the water and showed Boylan.

'Worms.'

Boylan took the worm off the hook, dipped it in his flask of Irish whiskey and handed it back to a puzzled looking Moylan.

'Try that?'

Moylan cast his line out and as soon as the worm hit the water, there was a great amount of splashing. His rod bent over and the line reeled out at an alarming rate.

'Have you got a bite?' asked Boylan.

'No,' shouted a struggling Moylan, 'but the worm's got a fish by the throat.'

An Irishman and his Swiss mountain guide, Toby le Rone, were caught in an avalanche. Thankfully they weren't hurt but they were firmly stuck in the snow. After a few hours a Saint Bernard came striding through the snow with a barrel of brandy tied under his chin.

'At last!' shouted Toby. 'Here comes man's best friend.'

'Aye,' said the Irishman, 'and would you look at the size of the dog bringing it.'

Did you hear the one about the Irishman who was sacked from his job at the 'M&M' sweet factory?
They sacked him for throwing all the Ws away!

✳ ✳ ✳ • ✳ ✳ ✳ • ✳ ✳ ✳

Police found a skeleton in a cupboard when they raided a house in Cork. After further investigations and detailed forensic tests, it was revealed that they had found the skeleton of Malley O'Scalley, Ireland's Hide and Seek World Champion from 1901.

✳ ✳ ✳ • ✳ ✳ ✳ • ✳ ✳ ✳

Did you hear the one about the Irish girl who wanted to buy a special pet?
    She asked the local petshop for a wasp and the shopkeeper said:
    'I'm sorry Miss. We don't sell wasps.'
    'But you've got one in the window!'

✳ ✳ ✳ • ✳ ✳ ✳ • ✳ ✳ ✳

Two Irishmen were sitting on the bus when one of them asked,
    'Why do you have a see-through lunch box?'
    'So when I'm sitting on the bus,' came the reply, 'I know whether I'm going to work or coming home.'

Two bird spotters, Bill and Ben were out at night looking for owls. It wasn't long before they heard the familiar hoots.

'Listen!' said Bill. 'Hear that...?'

Ben listened and heard, 'Twit Too Who.'

'That's a Barn Owl,' said Bill.

Just then they both heard a 'Whoo, Whoo.'

'And that's a Tawny Owl.'

It went quiet for a while then they both heard another call. 'That's an Irish Owl,' said Bill.

'How do you know?' asked Ben.

'Listen,' said Bill, and the Owl went, 'What? What?'

✳ ✳ ✳ • ✳ ✳ ✳ • ✳ ✳ ✳

Bernie and Bernadette spent Christmas in America and decided to go to a drive-in movie.

They found one and parked. After waiting for nearly 5 hours for the movie to start, Bernie was concerned.

'Are you sure there's a film on tonight?'

'Yes,' said Bernadette. 'There's a big sign back there advertising it.'

'What's it called?' asked Bernie.

'*Closed for the Winter*.'

An Irishman rang 999 in a panic.

'Can you help me?! My brother is lying on the floor unconscious.'

'What happened?' asked the operator.

'We were changing a light bulb...' the Irishman began.

'And did he receive an electric shock?' interrupted the operator.

'No, we were...'

'Did he fall off the ladder?' the operator interrupted again.

'No,' the Irishman said. 'In fact he wasn't up the ladder – I was. He was holding the ladder.'

'Well, how did he fall unconscious?'

'I think,' explained the Irishman, 'that he got dizzy spinning the ladder around for me, fell over and hit his head on the floor.'

Did you hear the one about the Irishman who climbed the chain link fence?
He wanted to see what was on the other side!

Two Irishmen were walking down a road when a lorry passed them carrying a load of rolled up turf.

'Now,' said one of them pointing to the lorry. 'That's what I would do if I had the money.'

'What's that?' asked the second.

'Send my lawn away to be cut.'

A man is on *Who wants to be a Millionaire* and is on the £500,000 question when Chris Tarrant asks him: 'What animal lives in a sett? Is it;

    A: A Rabbit

    B: A Cuckoo

    C: A Sheep

or

    D: A Badger?'

The man is not sure, so he goes 50/50. He's left with 'B: A Cuckoo' and 'D: A Badger.' He decides to 'phone a friend,' an Irish friend.

So, his Irish friend answers the phone and after hearing the question, very confidently says, 'D: A Badger.' The man asks if he's sure and the Irishman remains very confident. Sure enough, it's right, and the man wins! He walks away with half a million pounds.

The next day the two friends meet up for a celebratory drink.

'Hey, how come you were so sure of that answer last night. I had no idea.'

The Irishman said; 'Sure it was easy – everyone knows that a cuckoo lives in a clock.'

~~~~~~~~~~~~~~~~~~~~~~~~~~~~

A young Irish couple cuddled together one night after a romantic dinner and the boy said,

'I love you so much. I want to tell you everything that is in my heart.'

'Oh,' said the girl, 'that's so sweet, but just tell me everything that's in your head… It'll be quicker.'

'Well I think that was a successful trip,' said Captain Ahab O' Toole to a nearby sailor.

'We've been to Italy, Egypt, Turkey, Greece, Spain, Tunisia, Cyprus and Malta, all in eight days. I'd like to think that our passengers are more than satisfied with that, don't you think?'

'I don't think so, Captain,' replied the sailor.

'Why ever not?' asked the Captain.

'This is the Liverpool to Dublin ferry.'

A local Galway man was taking a stroll one Sunday afternoon when he came across a man in his sky-diving suit hanging from a tree.

'What happened to you?' asked the Galway man.

'I was sky-diving,' said the man, 'and my parachute failed to open.'

'You're not from round here, are you?' asked the Galway man.

'No,' replied the sky-diver. 'What's that got to do with it?'

'Well if you were a local man, you would know that round here, nothing opens on a Sunday.'

It was Halloween and an Irish chip shop owner was admitted to hospital with third-degree burns all over his face.

'What happened to you?' asked the Doctor.

'I was bobbing for chips,' he replied.

An Irish girl got a call from her mammy who had just moved into a new modern house.

'How is it Mammy?'

'Oh it's very nice,' said her mammy, 'but I don't like the new washing machine.'

'Why not?' asked the girl.

'Well I put 6 of your father's shirts into it, pulled the chain and never saw them again.'

✳ ✳ ✳ • ✳ ✳ ✳ • ✳ ✳ ✳

An Irishman wanted to take the car ferry. When he arrived at the terminal he saw the ferry about ten feet away from dock. Not wanting to miss it, he put his foot down and launched his car off the dockside. The car flew through the air, landing perfectly in a parking space on the ferry.

'How's that for a bit of driving,' said the proud Irishman to a nearby deckhand.

'It was great!' said the deckhand. 'But why didn't you wait? We were just about to dock.'

✳ ✳ ✳ • ✳

How do you keep an Irishman in suspense for hours?
Put him in front of a mirror and tell him to wait for the other person to say, 'Hello.'

An Englishman, a Scotsman and an Irishman stood before a firing squad. The Captain of the squad shouted, 'Ready... Aim...'

Suddenly the Englishman shouted, 'Earthquake!' The firing squad and the Captain were startled and as they looked around the Englishman escaped.

The Captain lined up the squad again and shouted, 'Ready... Aim...'

Suddenly the Scotsman shouted, 'Tornado!' Once again the firing squad and the Captain were startled. When they looked back, the Scotsman had already run away.

With only the Irishman left, the Captain lined up the squad once again and shouted, 'Ready... Aim...' The Irishman shouts, 'Fire!'

~~~~~~~~~~~~~~~~~~~~~~~~~~~

Two Irishmen were having a beer in the pub and chatting amiably.

'If you had a choice,' asked one, 'and you could have a conversation with anyone, living or dead, who would it be?'

'The living one,' the other Irishman replied quickly.

An Irishman went round to see his Mammy for a cup of tea. As his Mammy prepared the cups and kettle, the Irishman couldn't help noticing that every time his Mammy tip-toed past the medicine cabinet and kept very quiet.

'Mammy?' asked the Irishman. 'Why do you creep past that medicine cabinet?'

'I don't want to wake up the sleeping pills in there.'

An Irishman walks into a pub. The place is dead. No pool table, no dartboard, nothing, apart from a barman and a very pretty barmaid.

'What do you do for fun around here?' the Irishman asks the barman.

'I'll show you mate.'

The barman picks up a baseball bat and goes over to the corner of the pub where a gorilla is sitting and hits him over the head with the bat.

The gorilla goes crazy. It jumps all over that place, smashing tables and glasses, finally leaping over the bar to give the pretty barmaid a kiss.

'That's amazing!' says the Irishman. 'Especially when he kisses the barmaid.'

'Do you want a go?' asks the barman patting the bat.

'OK,' says the Irishman. 'But just don't hit me as hard.'

'How are the new false teeth?' one Irishwoman asked of another.

'Oh, they're not bad,' the other sighed, 'but I'm leaving them out until I get used to them.'

❋ ✳ ❋ • ❋ ✳ ❋ • ❋ ✳ ❋

An Irishwoman went into a fish and chip shop and asked for some fish and chips.

'Certainly,' said the man behind the counter, 'it won't be long.'

'Well make sure it's a fat one then,' said the Irishwoman.

❋ ✳ ❋ • ❋ ✳ ❋ • ❋ ✳ ❋

An Irishman went into his local bank.

'I'd like to speak to the person who arranges loans, please.'

'Sorry Sir, but the loan arranger isn't here,' replied the cashier.

'OK then,' he replied. 'I'll have a word with Tonto.'

❋ ✳ ❋ • ❋ ✳ ❋ • ❋ ✳ ❋

Did you hear the one about the vain Irishwoman who had too much plastic surgery?
She sat by her turf fire… and melted!

❋ ✳ ❋ • ❋ ✳ ❋ • ❋ ✳ ❋

Did you hear the one about the Irishman who threw away his brand new set of water skis?
He couldn't find a river that sloped!

A rich Irish businessman was talking to a reporter.

'When I came to Dublin from Cork,' he began, 'all I had were the clothes I stood up in, a pair of shoes with holes in them and the laces missing, and a stick over my shoulder with a bundle made out of an old used handkerchief hanging from the end of it. But soon I owned half the city. I also owned half the office blocks, three cinemas, twelve night clubs, at least thirty building sites, a film company, a taxi company and a collection of high quality restaurants.'

'That's amazing,' said the reporter. 'It just shows what hard work can do. Just one last question: what did you have in the bundle on the stick?'

'Oh, about 60 million Euro,' replied the businessman.

❋ ❋ ❋ ● ❋ ❋ ❋ ● ❋ ❋ ❋

It's a very well-known fact that the English invented the toilet seat in 1643. And very proud of it they were. Then in 1645, the Irish added the hole.

❋ ❋ ❋ ● ❋

Two Irishmen were running for the number 24, but just missed it.

'Oh Bejabers!' said the first Irishman. 'How are we going to get home now?'

'I know!' said the second Irishman. 'We'll wait for the number 12, and take it twice.'

An Irish girl was taking her driving test and had stalled the car.

'Now don't worry about that,' said the driving instructor.

'I'm sorry,' said the girl. 'I panicked.'

'It's OK; you're nervous,' the instructor said in calming tones.

'I didn't see the signs.' The Irish girl was very upset.

'No problem,' said the instructor. 'Just start the engine. Put the car in to first gear; indicate; check mirror and off we go.'

The Irish girl did as she was told. 'Which way shall we go?'
The instructor looked around. 'Well, if we go down this aisle, turn left at the meat counter, through the ten items only checkout and out the automatic doors we should get back to the car park.'

~~~~~~~~~~~~~~~~~~~~~~~~~~~~~~~~~~

AIRLINE ANNOUNCEMENTS
'The British Airways flight to New York will be leaving at eighteen-fifty-five. Thank you.'

'The Qantas flight to Sydney will be leaving at nineteen-oh-five. Thank you.'

'The Air France flight to Paris will be leaving at nineteen-forty. Thank you.'

'The Aer Lingus flight to Dublin will be leaving when the big hand is on the twelve and the little hand is on the eight. Thank you.'

Famous Irish jockey G.G. Ryder was leading the field during a race at Leopardstown when suddenly he got hit on the head with a frozen turkey and a box of Christmas crackers. He managed to keep on riding, then he was hit with a dozen mince pies and a Christmas pudding until he was finally knocked off his horse by a well-aimed jar of cranberry sauce.

At the end of the race, he complained to the stewards that he had been seriously hampered!

An Irishman went to the doctors with blisters all over his lips.

The doctor began his examination. 'That looks nasty. So, tell me how did you get those blisters on your lips?'

'Oh doctor,' said the Irishman. 'It always seems to happen after I've tried to blow out the light bulbs.'

Liam got a call from Shaun who was out in his new convertible sports car.

'What's up?' asked Liam.

'I've locked my keys in the car,' said Shaun.

'Oh don't worry,' said Liam. 'I'll just get a clothes hanger and we'll try to get in that way.'

'That's great,' said Shaun, 'but would you hurry up? It looks like rain and I've got the top down.'

An Irishman was filling up a bucket with fish from a private river.

'Right, caught you red-handed,' said the gamekeeper. 'Poaching fish from private property.'

'I'm not poaching,' said the Irishman.

'Don't try and talk your way out of this. You've a got a bucket of fish there.'

The Irishman looked in the bucket. 'Oh these aren't poached. They're my pet fish from my pond at home and I often bring them up here for a swim, then we go back home.'

'I don't believe you,' said the gamekeeper. So the Irishman emptied the bucket into the river and the fish swam away. After about an hour no fish had returned.

The gamekeeper finally laughed. 'See, I knew you were lying. Where are your fish now?'

'What fish?' said the Irishman.

❋ ✳ ❋ • ❋ ✳ ❋ • ❋ ✳ ❋

An Irishman was up in court in front of the judge for not paying maintenance money to his ex-wife. The judge, as a punishment decided to increase the Irishman's payments.

'Mr Finnegan I have decided to increase this allowance and give your ex-wife 75 pounds a week.'

The Irishman smiled.

'Thank you M'lud. You are a gentleman. I tell you what, I might even send her a bob or two myself.'

The English Captain of a Royal Navy ship received a radio call from Paddy.

'Please alter your course 43 degrees to the West to avoid a collision.'

The Captain replied. 'Suggest you change your course to 43 degrees East to avoid a collision.'

'Ah now, I can't be doing that,' said Paddy calmly. 'So please alter your course 43 degrees to the West to avoid a collision.'

'I am the Captain of a Royal Naval Aircraft carrier and I say alter your course.'

'And I say again,' replied Paddy, 'You should steer her over a bit.'

The Captain was furious. 'Good God man, I am the Captain of Britain's biggest aircraft carrier with enough firepower to blast you out of the water. Who on earth are you?'

'I'm Paddy.'

'Paddy who?' shouted the Captain.

'Paddy the lighthouse keeper. Please alter your course.'

✳ ✳ ✳ • ✳

Did you hear about the Irish boy who ate all the Christmas decorations off the tree?
He's OK now, but he was rushed to hospital with Tinselitus!

Colleen met a very sad Nolleen coming out of the vet's.

'What's the matter?' Colleen asked.

'The vet has just told me that I have killed my new Toy Poodle,' said Nolleen tearfully.

'What did you do?' questioned Colleen.

'Nothing much, I just tried to put in new batteries.'

An Irishman was in his local pub supping his pint of stout when his wife burst in.

'I thought I'd find you here!' she shouted. 'You spend more time in this pub than you do at home with me. Why do you come here so much and…'

She took a sip of his stout.

'Urgh! And drink this awful stuff?'

'And you thought I was out enjoying myself,' replied the Irishman.

An Irishman applied for a job as a handyman in a Dublin hotel. The manager conducted the interview:

'So, can you do electrical work?'

'Er, no,' said the Irishman.

'Oh, what about plumbing?'

'Sorry, Sir, I can't do that either.'

'Right, what about carpentry?'

'Ah now, that's something with wood, isn't it? I can't do that either.'

'You can't do electrical work, can't do plumbing, or carpentry! Why did you apply for the job?'

'But I'm handy – I only live next door.'

An Irishman went into a fishmonger's.

'I'd like a pair of kippers for the wife, please.'

'I'm sorry, Sir,' said the fishmonger, 'we haven't got a pair left.'

'Oh, just give me two odd ones,' said the Irishman. 'She'll never notice.'

Three friends, an Englishman, an American and an Irishman went to a local Beer Festival. They went to the busy World beer tent and ordered their drinks.

'I'd like the best beer in the world,' said the American. 'Give me a Budweiser.'

The Englishman was next.

'Actually, I would like the best beer in the world, please. Please may I have a pint of English Best Bitter?'

'And what would you like?' the barman asked the Irishman.

'I'd like orange juice, please.'

The American and Englishman are shocked.

'Why aren't you having a Guinness?'

'Well, I thought, if you weren't drinking, then I wouldn't either.'

Two Irishmen were discussing their childhood.

'When I was younger, I had two half brothers and a half sister,' one of the Irishmen reminisced. 'Then my Da took the chainsaw away from me.'

A gorilla walks into a Belfast pub and asks for a pint of best.

'Certainly Sir,' says the barman but as it's a gorilla, he decides to over-charge him.

'That'll be five pounds please.'
The gorilla opens his wallet and hands over a five-pound note. The barman takes the money.

'I hope you don't mind me saying, but we don't get a lot of talking gorillas in Belfast.'

'At five pounds a pint, I'm not surprised!'

A man went to his local pet shop to return a cat he had bought a few weeks ago.

'When I bought that cat from you,' he said to the Irish pet shop owner, 'you said it was good for mice. Well let me tell you, this cat doesn't catch mice.'

'Well,' said the Irish pet shop owner.

'That's good for the mice then, isn't it?'

Did you hear the one about the little Irish boy who went to the cinema?
The girl on the ticket counter said that he couldn't get in because the film was an 18 and over only. He spent the rest of the afternoon finding 17 more friends to go with him.

Thaddy went round to see Paddy and saw him lying on the floor in a pool of sweat in the middle of a freshly painted room. He noticed that Paddy was wearing a donkey jacket, under a woollen top and hood.

'Are you OK?' asks Thaddy.

'Oh I'm fine,' says Paddy, 'just doing some painting. It got a bit hot and I think I passed out.'

'I'm not surprised,' said Thaddy. 'Why are you wearing that jacket and woollen top?'

'Just following directions,' said Paddy, showing Thaddy the instructions on the paint tin. 'For best results, put on two coats.'

❋ ❋ ❋ • ❋ ❋ ❋ • ❋ ❋ ❋

A stranger walks into a Cork pub.

'I will give anyone here £100 if they can drink ten pints of stout in ten minutes.'

No one takes him up on the offer, but he does see Brophy leave the pub. A little while later Brophy returns to the pub, and asks the stranger if the bet is still on.

The stranger says it is, so Brophy takes the bet. Nine minutes later Brophy has drunk ten pints of stout.

'Well done,' says the stranger, handing over the hundred pounds. 'But tell me, where did you go when you left the pub earlier?'

'Oh,' said Brophy, 'I went down the road to the other pub to see if I could do it.'

Two Irishmen were walking past a cornfield. Out in the middle they saw another Irishman rowing a boat.

'Would ye look at that eejit,' said one of the Irishmen. 'It's people like that that give the Irish a bad name and makes everyone think we're stupid.'

'I know,' said his friend. 'And if I knew how to swim, I'd go out there and tip him out.'

~~~~~~~~~~~~~~~~

Crash investigators were questioning the Irishman as he lay in a hospital bed after he had crashed his helicopter.

'So can you tell us what happened?' asked one of the officials.

'It's all a blur,' said the Irishman. 'All I can remember is that one minute I was flying along and was feeling a bit cold, so I decided to turn that big overhead fan off...'

~~~~~~~~~~~~~~~~

An Irishman went into a pub and ordered a Martini. When it came, he took the olive out and put it in a small jar he was carrying. He then ordered another one and did the same thing with the olive. He kept doing this all evening until the jar was filled with olives, then staggered away from the bar. He was just about to leave when the barman called out to him.

'Excuse me. I couldn't help noticing what you were doing. What was that all about?'

'Oh nothing,' slurred the Irishman. 'The missus sent me out for a jar of olives.'

'Why are you late for work?' asked the Irish girl's boss.

'I'm sorry,' said the Irish girl, 'but I was using the escalator at the station. There was a power cut and I was stranded for nearly an hour.'

An Irishman returned home to see his brand new car in the living room.

'How on earth did that get there?' he screamed in horror.

'Easy,' his wife said. 'I just turned right at the kitchen.'

Did you hear the one about the shy Irish academic who went into the university library?
He took out a very big book out called *How to Hug*. When he got it back to his room he found out that it was volume seven of a set of encyclopaedias.

Did you hear the one about the Irish couple who went away for a camping weekend?
Unfortunately, they pitched their tent right in the middle of a cow field. That night the cows attacked them. It wasn't too serious; the boy got away with a few bruises, but the girl was badly grazed.

A stranger was surrounded by a gang of Irish boys, the leader of which gave him a dice and said,

'I want you to throw that dice and if it lands on 1, 2 or 3, we're going to beat you up with our fists. But if it lands on 4 or 5 we're gong to beat you up with our boots.'

'W… W… What if I throw a six?' stammered the stranger.

The leader smiled. 'Then you get another go.'

Lying on his back looking up at the millions and millions of stars that lit up the night sky like a scattering of diamonds on a velvet drape, the Irishman thought to himself, 'The stars, the stars, what is the stars?' and then after a little while…

'I wonder who's nicked my tent?'

The police arrested O'Malley who was drunk on battery acid and O'Shalley who thought he was a firework. They put them both in a cell overnight. In the morning they charged O'Malley and let O'Shalley off.

Two Irish hippies were talking to each other at a rock concert.

The first hippie asks, 'Hey bro, what would you do if you saw a spaceman?'

And the second hippie said, 'To be sure, I'd park me car in it.'

Did you hear about the unlucky Irishman?
It started off when he was born. He was an only child and still wasn't Daddy's favourite. In fact his Dad tried to claim the birth against his accident insurance.
He got a letter from *Reader's Digest* telling him that he hadn't reached the final round of the draw.
He peeled a banana once and it was empty.
He bought a duck and it sank.
He had a swimming pool and it burnt down.

❋ ❋ ❋ ● ❋ ❋ ❋ ● ❋ ❋ ❋

An Irish priest was driving home one night and was weaving all across the road. The police stopped him and asked if he had been drinking.

'Just from this bottle of water,' said the priest. The policeman took the bottle and sniffed it.

'This isn't water,' he said, 'it's wine.'

'It's a miracle!' exclaimed the priest.

❋ ❋ ❋ ● ❋

'I've just received a fax from our Irish branch,' said the secretary to her boss. The boss examined the fax.

'How do you know it's from our Irish branch? There's no address on it.'

'I know,' said the secretary, 'but it does have a stamp on it.'

An Irishman had drunk far too much and was wandering about trying to find out where he lived. Finally he got fed up and hailed a taxi.

'Take me to 46 Sally Gardens,' he slurred as he collapsed into the back seat.

The taxi driver looked about.

'You drunken fool, you're outside 46 Sally Gardens!'

'Right!' said the Irishman. 'And the next time, don't drive so fast.'

~~~~~~~~~~~~~~~~~~~~~~~~~~~~~

Liam and Shaun are sitting in front of the television watching the ten o'clock news, which is showing an item about a man threatening to jump off the roof of an office block in Dublin.

Liam says to Shaun, 'I bet you £25 that he jumps!'

'£25?' says Shaun. 'Make it £50 and you've got a bet.'

Liam agrees and they shake hands on the bet and continue watching. Sure enough, the man jumps and lands on the firemen's safety sheet on the road below. Shaun takes £50 out of his wallet and hands it to Liam.

'I can't take your money, mate,' Liam says. 'I was cheating. I saw this on the six o'clock news, so I knew he was going to jump.'

'No, fair's fair,' says Shaun. 'That money is yours. In fact it was me who was cheating as I saw it on the five o'clock news, but I just didn't think he would do it again.'

An Irishwoman had gone out for a drive in the brand new family car. After a while she rang her husband at home.

'Darling, I've got some news about the car. It's good news and then again it isn't.'

'What's the good news?' asked her husband nervously.

'The air bag works,' she shrilled.

Two IT experts were talking one day.

'Of course you know the difference between a computer and an Irishman?'

'No?' said his colleague.

'Well,' said the first IT expert, 'you only have to give the information to a computer once.'

Bob and Betty Dolley had a lovely holiday in Greece.

'They have lovely beaches,' Betty told her neighbour. 'Me and Bob had a great time burying each other in that soft golden sand.'

'Are you going again next year?' asked the neighbour.

'I think I might. I might even dig Bob up this time and bring him home with me.'

Mary couldn't help but notice that her friend had a black eye and a bandage wrapped around her head.

'Colleen, what happened to your face?'

'Oh,' said Colleen, 'I was putting some of that fancy toilette water on my face.'

'And?'

'Well, the lid fell down on my head.'

❋ ❋ ❋ • ❋ ❋ ❋ • ❋ ❋ ❋

An Irishman returned home from the pub one night to a torrent of abuse from his wife.

'If you spent as much time at home, as you spend in that pub,' she moaned, 'I think I'd fall down dead.'

'There now,' said the Irishman, 'there'll be no use you trying to bribe me.'

❋ ❋ ❋ • ❋ ❋ ❋ • ❋ ❋ ❋

Kerry and Terry were playing golf, when Kerry sliced his ball into the branches of a gigantic oak on one side of the green.

'Dat's unplayable,' said Terry. 'Dat's a penalty stroke.'

'No dat's alroight,' said Kerry. 'I think I can get dat. I got a tree iron in me bag.'

❋ ❋ ❋ • ❋ ❋ ❋ • ❋ ❋ ❋

Sir Dinsmore Kildare the famous Irish theatre actor was directing his first stage play, but he wasn't very happy with an actor's death-bed scene.

'Dear boy!' he bellowed in theatrical tones. 'Could you please put some more life into your dying.'

An Irish steamroller driver came rushing into the bar shouting.

'Hey, can anyone tell me how tall a penguin is?'

'About two foot six,' said the barman.

'Oh, begorah!' cried the Irishman. 'I've just run over a nun.'

A man walked into the pub with a small and cute puppy under his arm.

'What a nice looking dog!' said his Irish friend.

'Yeah,' smiled the man. 'I got it for the wife.'

'Seems like a fair swap,' replied the Irishman.

Now I'm not saying that she is the biggest woman in Ireland, but last week she bent over in Wexford and they had an eclipse in Kerry!

An Irishman presented his wife with a diamond ring for her birthday.

'Wow!' said his impressed wife. 'Is it a real diamond?'

'I hope so,' said the Irishman, 'otherwise that bloke in the pub has swindled me out of two pounds fifty.'

An Irishman was broken-hearted over his girlfriend.

'Why won't you marry me?' he asked as the tears ran down his face. Then he suddenly became suspicious. 'Is there someone else?'

'Oh, bejabers,' she sighed. 'There must be.'

Mick O'Mouse was a strange man on account of being born with two left feet. Most of the time it was fine, but when he went on holiday and he wanted something to wear on the beach, he spent hours in shoe shops looking for a pair of 'Flip-Flips'.

An Irish girl went in to see her Boss.

'Excuse me sir,' she said.

'What is it?' asked the Boss.

'You know that letter you asked me to write double-spaced?'

'Yes?'

'Well I was just wondering, do you want the photocopies double-spaced as well?'

It's a well-known fact that an Englishman laughs at a joke at least three times:

Once when everybody he is with, gets it; the second time a week later when he thinks he gets it; and about a month later when an Irishman explains it to him.

Did you hear about the Irish woodworm?
It was found in a brick!

Two pilots were walking round a military airfield and one was pointing out all the different helicopters.

'See that one over there? That's an American Helicopter. You can tell by all the computers it has fitted on board.'

He then points to another one. 'And that one is a Russian Helicopter: the tell-tale sign is the type of missiles it has fitted.'

'What about that one over there?' the other pilot asked, pointing to another helicopter.

'Oh, that's an Irish Helicopter.'

'How do you know this time?' asked the second pilot.

'It's the only one fitted with an ejector seat.'

'Bridey, have you seen my new vest?' Dougal asked his wife.

'Oh yer big eejit, Dougal,' said Bridey. 'You're wearing it!'

'Oh thank God you noticed that,' said Dougal, 'otherwise I would have gone out without it.'

Two Irishmen were out shooting ducks. One of them took aim, fired, missed and hit a pigeon. The unfortunate bird fell from the sky and landed at their feet. One of them looked at the remains.

'Oh dear, you should have saved the bullet.'

'It's OK,' replied the other Irishman. 'The fall would have killed him anyway.'

❋ ✳ ❋ • ❋ ✳ ❋ • ❋ ✳ ❋

An Irishman went to Dublin to change his name. He went to the appropriate department and the clerk asked what his name was. 'Michael O'Hairy,' he said.

'I see,' said the clerk trying not to laugh. 'And what do you want it changed to?'

'Ernie.'

❋ ✳ ❋ • ❋ ✳ ❋ • ❋ ✳ ❋

Two teams of Irish workmen were putting up telegraph poles. At the end of the day the site manager called the teams in.

'Well done lads,' he said. 'But I want to ask just one question to the foreman of the second team.'

'What's that Sir?' said the foreman of the second team.

'Well, I was just wondering why your team only put in two telegraph poles all day, when the other team did twenty?'

'Ah now, that was because they were cheating,' said the foreman. 'Did you see how much they left sticking out of the ground?'

Two Irish girls were talking about the new nightclub that had opened in town.

'I went there last night. It was packed to the roof. The dance floor was full, the bar was full – even the staircase was full. You can understand why nobody goes there.'

❋ * ❋ • ❋ * ❋ • ❋ * ❋

An Irishman arrived at Shannon Airport and wandered around the terminal in tears. Finally an airline official went up to him to ask what the matter was.

'I've lost all my luggage,' wept the Irishman.

'Oh dear,' said the official. 'What happened?'

'The cork fell out!' sobbed the Irishman.

❋ * ❋ • ❋ * ❋ • ❋ * ❋

A man was walking through a park when he saw two Irishmen digging. One was digging holes and the other one was busy filling them in again.

'Excuse me,' called the man. 'What are you doing?'

'Well,' said the Irishman digging the holes, 'there are generally three of us on this job. Me, Marley and Farley. I dig the holes, Marley puts the new trees in and Farley there fills in the holes. Marley has the flu.'

An Irishman had bought his first ever video player. He went to the video shop and in his excitement picked up the first video he saw and took it home. He put it in the player, settled down to watch the video. Unfortunately there was nothing but static on the screen and no matter how the Irishman played with the controls, he couldn't see a thing. He rang up the video shop and told them his problem.

'I'm sorry about that, Sir. Please bring it back and we shall exchange it.'

'Thanks,' said the Irishman and was about to put the phone down when the video shop clerk spoke.

'By the way, Sir, what's was the name of the video?'

The Irishman looked at the box, '*Head Cleaner*.'

Irish scientists have discovered that we only use a quarter of our brain power.

They are still trying to discover what do we do with the other quarter!

'Is that Interpol?' said the Irish voice on the phone.

'Oui,' replied the French officer.

'Can you send a bunch of roses to me Mammy?'

Two Irishmen were flying home from a Drinks convention when the captain of the plane announced that one of the engines had failed, but that they had three left. Everything was all right, but the flight would take an hour longer. A little while later the captain announced that another engine had failed, but that they had two left and that everything would be all right. The flight would now take two hours longer.

Not long after that the captain announced that a third engine had failed. Everything was all right, but the flight would now take four hours longer.

At this point one of them turned pale and said, 'I hope the last engine doesn't fail, otherwise we'll be up here all day.'

An Irishman went into an electrical shop in London and said to the assistant, 'I'd like to buy that television please.'

'I'm sorry,' said the assistant. 'Company policy: we're not allowed to serve Irishmen.'

Upset but not defeated, the Irishman went home, put on a wig, a false nose, some glasses and a suit and went back to shop and asked in an English accent.

'Here mate, I wanna buy that television, aw-right?'

'Look I'm sorry, but it's company policy: I'm not allowed to serve any Irishmen.'

'But how did you know I was Irish?' asked the Irishman disappointed.

'Because,' sneered the assistant, 'the television you want is a microwave.'

Not many people realise that an Irishman invented the first electric car. It went from Dublin to Belfast on only £10 worth of electricity. It never caught on though, because the extension lead cost over £25,000.

An Irishman was so desperate to get in to see the big match that he pushed in front of people waiting to get their tickets. A steward stopped him and told him to go to the back of the queue. Off the Irishman went but was back again very soon trying to push in.

'Oy!' said the steward. 'I thought I told you to go to the back of the queue.'

'I did,' said the Irishman, 'but there was already somebody there.'

Did you hear about the Irish Tooth Fairy?
She was sacked for leaving the tooth under the pillow and taking all the other teeth!

It was Nola's birthday and Nolan was being a considerate husband.

'I'm going to get you a big – no, a large – no, an enormous – no, a mega-enormous box of chocolates for your birthday,' he told Nola.

'But you know I'm on a diet!'

'I used to have a great variety act,' said Patrick O'Hattrick the retired Irish entertainer when he was being interviewed on TV.

'I had a parrot that could imitate famous film stars of the time. You name it, that parrot could imitate it. He could even walk like John Wayne and dance like Fred Astaire. Unfortunately though, we didn't get enough work. I was penniless and hungry so I had to eat him.'

'You had to eat your parrot?' said the shocked interviewer. 'What did it taste like?'

'Roast beef,' said Patrick. 'Like I said that parrot could imitate anything.'

❋ ❋ ❋ • ❋ ❋ ❋ • ❋ ❋ ❋

Two priests were talking about Irish weddings.

'Of course you can always tell who the bride is when you're doing an Irish country wedding,' said one.

'How?' asked the second priest.

'She's the one wearing the white Wellington boots.'

❋ ❋ ❋ • ❋

'Nolan, do you think I'm getting crows' feet?' asked Nola as they prepared to go out for the evening.

'You might be,' said Nolan. 'Just keep your shoes on tonight and no one will notice.'

An Irishman came home from a hard day planting potatoes and talked to his wife.

'Just for a change, instead of just defrosting frozen food and putting in the microwave to cook, couldn't we have a traditional home-cooked meal?'

'Of course you can,' said his wife. 'I'll just open some tins.'

'You don't deserve a wife like me!' screamed the Irishwoman at her husband during a row.

'I don't deserve toothache either,' moaned the Irishman, 'but I've got it.'

Patrick became a monk and joined an order where he was only allowed to speak once every five years. At the end of the first five years the Abbot told Patrick that he could speak one sentence.

'The beds are very hard here,' he said.

Ten years later the Abbot allowed him another sentence.

'Can we do something about the beds, they're very uncomfortable?' asked Patrick.

Fifteen years later it was Patrick's time to speak again.

'You've still done nothing about the beds and my back is killing me.'

Twenty years later when the time came to speak Patrick stood up and said to the Abbot,

'Right! That's it! I'm leaving this order.'

'Good!' snapped the Abbot. 'You've done nothing but complain since you got here.'

A dance instructor thought he could dance every dance there was. Then he heard about the 'Irish Butcher Dance.' Eager to learn this dance he travelled to Ireland to seek out the only 'Irish Butcher Dance' instructor, who told him that lessons would cost £750,000. So desperate was the dance instructor to learn it, that he sold his house, his car and most of his clothes to raise the money. He borrowed from the bank and loan sharks. He ate very little and never went out and finally had enough money. Handing the money over to the instructor, the now penniless man could hardly wait for his first lesson.

'OK, here we go,' said the Irish dance instructor.

'Butcher right foot in, Butcher right foot out, in, out, in, out, yer shake it all about.'

A boy asked his Irish girlfriend what she would like for St Valentine's Day.

'Do you like Chanel No 5?' he asked.

'Not really,' said the Irish girl, 'but there are some good programmes on ITV.'

Did you hear the one about the Irishman who was killed while drinking milk?
The cow fell on him!

The Irish Mountain Climbing team were in a spot of trouble, hanging off a cliff face holding onto a single rope.

'It's no good lads!' the leader shouted. 'There's ten of us holding on here and the rope won't hold – it'll snap. Someone has got to let go of the rope, so that nine of us will stand a chance of survival.'

Big Paddy shouted up from the bottom of the rope.

'I'll do it Boss. I'm the heaviest.'

'Thanks Paddy, and God be with you.'

Big Paddy let go of the rope and fell to his certain death.

'There goes a brave man,' said the leader.

'OK everyone: round of applause for Big Paddy.'

❋ ❋ ❋ • ❋ ❋ ❋ • ❋ ❋ ❋

Miss O'Grundy was standing up in front of her class giving an English lesson.

'Now class,' she said, 'consider this sentence: "I didn't have no fun this weekend."'

'Who can tell me how I should correct this?'

Little Patrick put his hand up and said, 'Get a boyfriend, Miss.'

❋ ❋ ❋ • ❋ ❋ ❋ • ❋ ❋ ❋

A photographer met with a beautiful Irish model.

'Would you mind if I photographed you in the nude?'

'Not at all,' she said. 'But won't you be cold? This studio is very draughty.'

Farmer O'Toole had been invited round to supper by his neighbour, Farmer O'Giles.

Knowing they both liked a drink or six, and that it would be dark on the walk home, O'Toole took a big stable lantern with him. Sure enough, the farmers drank heartily and O'Toole set off home guided by his lantern.

The next day Farmer O'Giles rang.

'Did you get home alright last night?' he asked.

'Oh I did,' said O'Toole.

'Oh good,' said O'Giles, 'because you left your lantern here.'

'Did I?' asked puzzled O'Toole. 'But how did I get home?'

'I don't know,' replied O'Giles. 'Could I have my parrot and cage back please?'

❋ ❋ ❋ • ❋ ❋ ❋ • ❋ ❋ ❋

An Irish teenager was standing on the corner having a sly cigarette when an elderly lady came up to him.

'Does your Mammy know you smoke?' she snapped. The teenager took another puff, 'Does your husband know you speak to strange men?'

Two Irish bird spotters were looking at something through their binoculars.

'And I say it's a magpie. It's got all the right markings and it's black and white.'

'It's not a magpie,' said the second spotter. 'It's a black-headed gull.'

'It's a magpie.'

'It's a black-headed gull.'

'It's a magpie.'

'It's a black-headed gull.'

This went on for quite a while until another Irish bird spotter came up to ask what they were arguing about. They told him; so he had a look through his binoculars.

'You're both wrong,' he said. 'It's a Friesian cow.'

The young Irish lad went round to his girlfriend's house to talk to her father about their plans.

'I'd like to ask you for your daughter's hand in marriage.'

The father thought for a moment.

'You'll take all of her, or nothing.'

The manager of the Dublin to Wicklow train was fed up with the last carriage always being vandalised. It was a porter at Dublin station that finally came up with the idea of leaving the last carriage off the train.

'Is that O'Riley's Sign Writers?' shouted an angry voice down the phone.

'Yes it is,' answered O'Riley. 'How can I help you?'

'I'm Farmer McDonald and that eejit you sent round to paint the name of my farm has made a right mess of it. He's spelt "farm" wrong.'

'Oh dear,' said O'Riley. 'Did he put the "A" and the "R" round the wrong way?'

'No!' screamed the farmer. 'He spelt it E.I.E.I.O!'

An old Irish lady got onto a very busy bus, looking very tired and harassed. A young boy stood up.

'You look tired. Would you like to sit in my seat for a while?'

'Oh no thank you,' she said. 'I'm in too much of a hurry to sit down.'

An Irish girl was chatting to another girl at a party.

'Hey, do you see that fella over there? He is so ugly! Looks like he fell out of the ugly tree and hit every branch on the way down. He'd make a good monster in a movie, and he wouldn't need any make up either.'

'Do you know who I am?' the girl asked.

'No,' said the Irish girl.

'I'm that fella's girlfriend.'

'Oh? Do you know who I am?'

'No!' snapped the girl.

'Good,' said the Irish girl and ran off.

An Irishman went into a chemist and asked for some rat poison.

'I'm sorry, Sir,' said the chemist. 'We don't sell rat poison. Have you tried Boots?'

'I want to poison them, yer eejit,' replied the Irishman, 'not kick them to death!'

✳ ✳ ✳ ● ✳ ✳ ✳ ● ✳ ✳ ✳

An Irishman was house-, pet- and granny-sitting for a family who had gone away on holiday. When the family returned the Dad asked how things were.

'Your cat is dead,' he said and the children started to cry.

'Nice one,' said the Dad to the Irishman. 'Couldn't you have been more tactful?'

'What do you mean?' asked the Irishman.

'Well you could have said something like, the cat was up on the roof when it slipped and fell to ground. You did all you could for it, but it died on the way to the vets.'

'Oh,' said the Irishman. 'I'll remember next time.'

'That's OK,' said the Dad. 'So how is granny?'

'Well,' started the Irishman, 'she was up on the roof and...'

An Irishman had almost got the job as chief teaspoon stirrer on the building site, when the boss said he wanted to give him an intelligence test.

'What has one thumb, four fingers and is sometimes made of leather?' asked the boss.

The Irishman thought long and hard before finally giving up.

'It's a glove,' said the boss. 'OK let's try another one. What has two thumbs, eight fingers and is made of leather?'

The Irishman thought even longer and harder and once again gave up.

'It's two gloves.' The boss nearly snapped. 'Look, I'll give you one more chance.'

'OK, I'll definitely get this one,' the Irishman said.

'This one is easy. Who is the Queen of England?'

The Irishman smiled. He knew this one all right.

'Now, that would be three gloves.'

✳ ✳ ✳ • ✳

The Doctor was amazed after he had examined an Irishman, who had come in complaining of stomach pains.

'You're not going to believe this,' said the doctor, 'but you're pregnant.'

'You're joking!' replied the Irishman, a man in his forties. 'What will the neighbours say? I'm not even married!'

Two Irishmen bought a tandem together, and they were out on their first ride. Everything was going well until they came to a very steep hill. The one on the back pedalled as hard as he could to reach top of the hill.

'That was a steep hill!' the Irishman said to his friend between gasping for breath.

'I know,' said the second Irishman. 'And it was lucky I kept the brakes on going up, otherwise we might have slid all the way back down it.'

~~~~~~~~~~~~~~~~~~~~

Finnegan Beginnegan got a job painting the white lines in the middle of the road. At the end of his third day he was called into the manager's office.

'Now tell me Finnegan,' said the manager. 'How is it you painted three miles of lines on your first day, one mile on your second day, and less than 100 yards today?'

'It's not an easy job you know, boss,' said Finnegan, 'because each day it takes longer to walk back to the paint pot.'

~~~~~~~~~~~~~~~~~~~~

There was a knock on an Irishman's front door and he opened it to see a man with some leaflets and a Bible.

'Excuse me, Sir,' the man said, 'but would you like to become a Jehovah's Witness?'

'Oh I don't think so,' said the Irishman. 'I didn't even see the accident.'

An Irishman went to catch a bus and before he got on he asked the conductor how much it was to the High Street.

'£1.50,' the conductor said.

The Irishman thought that was far too expensive, so he ran behind the bus to save the pennies. After a couple of stops, he called to the conductor again and asked how much it was to the High Street.

'£3,' said the conductor.

'£3?' said the Irishman. 'But it was only £1.50 when I last asked.'

'This bus is going the other way.'

An Irishman had never played golf before, but he was invited by a business colleague to play at an exclusive club. On the first tee, he took a couple of practice swings then hit the ball.

The ball sailed through the air and went straight in the hole. On the second tee, he belted the ball and got a hole in one again. He did it yet again on the third and fourth hole. On the fifth he hit the ball and sliced it widely. The ball hit some trees, bounced back out and hit a passing golf buggy, fell on to the green, rolled past the hole and up the green, then trickled back and plopped into the hole.

'Oh bejabers,' said the Irishman to his stunned partner. 'I thought I'd missed it that time.'

An Irishman was on holiday in Devon when he saw farmer loading up a truck with manure.

'What are you going to do with that?' the Irishman asked.

'I's gonna spread it on me strawberries,' said the farmer.

'Cor, you English are strange,' laughed the Irishman. 'We like cream on ours.'

❋ ❋ ❋ ● ❋ ❋ ❋ ● ❋ ❋ ❋

An Irish priest walked into his church and saw a little girl sitting in one of the pews crying.

'What's the matter sweetheart?' asked the priest. The little girl pointed up to the sky and sobbed.

'My Mammy and Da are up there and they've left me all alone!'

'Oh don't worry, child,' said the priest in reassuring tones. 'They are with the angels.'

'No they're not!' said the little girl. 'They're stripping the lead off the roof.'

❋ ❋ ❋ ● ❋ ❋ ❋ ● ❋ ❋ ❋

Two old Irishmen were sitting on a park bench having a chat about their hearing aids.

'The one I'm wearing is a state of the art digital sound enhancement system, with a range of half a mile, it doesn't hiss and can receive signals in 5.1 surround sound and Dolby logic. If you flick a switch you can even pick up the radio,' one of them said.

'That's amazing,' said the other Irishman. 'How much did it cost?'

'Half past three,' replied the old man.

The doctor rang an Irishwoman to see how she was doing with the pills he had prescribed for her bad back.

'Oh not too bad, doctor,' she said, 'but I do have a bit of a problem.'

'What's that?' asked the doctor.

'On the label it says take once after a bath.'

'That's right,' said the doctor. 'What's the problem?'

'Well,' said the Irishwoman. 'It's very tough going drinking all that bath water.'

✻ ✳ ✻ • ✻ ✳ ✻ • ✻ ✳ ✻

'That's a strange looking dog,' Shamus said to the Stranger who came into the bar. 'What is it?'

'It's a long-nosed, long-tailed, short-legged terrier,' said the Stranger.

'I bet you £50 that my dog here could beat yours in a fight,' said Shamus, indicating the large Wolfhound that sat at his feet.

The Stranger took up the offer and the fight began. Within seconds Shamus's Wolfhound was dead.

'Wow, that dog can fight!' said Shamus, handing over the money. 'What did you say it was called?'

'A long-nosed, long-tailed, short-legged terrier.' replied the Stranger. 'But some people call it a crocodile.'

An Irishman was trying to make his own cider.

'How's it going?' asked his mate.

'Not too bad,' replied the Irishman, 'but it's a heck of a job squeezing the juice out of the woodpeckers.'

An Irishman had joined the army and was in the queue to get his kit.

'I don't know any of my sizes. I'm going to look a right eejit.'

'Don't worry,' said the guy in front. 'You're a little bit bigger than me, so when I say a measurement, you just say the next number.'

The Quartermaster snapped at the guy and the Irishman in turn.

'Boots?'

'Seven,' said the guy.

'Eight,' said the Irishman.

'Trousers?'

'Thirty-four,' said the guy.

'Thirty-five,' said the Irishman.

'Shirt collar?'

'Fourteen,' said the guy.

'Fifteen,' said the Irishman.

'And finally hat size!' the Quartermaster bellowed.

'Six and seven-eighths,' said the guy.

'Nine, ten, eleven,' said the Irishman.

An Irishman was queuing up at a ticket office in a train station.

'I'd like a return ticket please.'

'Where to?' asked the ticket sales woman.

'Back here, you stupid woman!' replied the Irishman.

'My granddad was burnt in a fire yesterday,' an upset Irishman told his friend.

'Was it bad?' he asked.

The Irishman wiped a tear from his eye. 'They don't mess about at that crematorium.'

'My husband never takes me out,' the Irishwoman moaned to her friend.

'Why ever not?' asked her friend.

'He says that it would be wrong of him to be seen out with a married woman.'

Mary opens her newspaper one morning and is surprised to see that according to the obituary column, she had died a few days ago. Dumbfounded, she phones up Colleen.

'Have you read the paper today?' Mary asks.

'No.'

'Well it says in there that I've died!' Mary shrieks.

'Are you sure?' questions Colleen.

'Of course I'm sure!'

There's a short silence on the phone and then...

'So Mary, where *are* you calling from?'

After months of planning and scheming, an Irishman had to give up his idea of robbing the local bank.
No matter how hard he tried, the tights only came up to his neck.

An English kid, a Scottish laddie and an Irish scallywag came across an enchanted playground. They knew it was enchanted because there was a leprechaun looking after it.

'The slide is a magical slide,' the leprechaun declared. 'Whatever you shout out as you slide down, will be at the bottom when you arrive.

The English kid went first and shouted out 'Playstations.'

And sure enough he landed in amongst a gigantic pile of Playstations and games.

The Scottish laddie went next and he shouted out 'DVDs' and he landed in a big pile of DVDs.

Finally it was the turn of the Irish scallywag. He climbed to the top of the ladder, full of ideas. As he slid down, he screamed at the top of his voice.

'Weeeeeeee!'

'Did you hear about the Irishman who bought a house boat?'

'Really?'

'He drowned last week.'

'What happened?'

'He tried to add a basement.'

An Irishwoman was nearing the end of her life. As her husband comforted her on her deathbed she had some wise words for him.

'You've been a wonderful husband to me. When I'm gone I want you to find another woman, get married and enjoy yourself. In fact I'd like you to give your new wife all my old clothes, especially my expensive dresses.'

'Darling, that's a wonderful gesture,' whispered the husband. 'But I can't do that!'

'I understand,' said the Irishwoman.

'No you don't,' said the husband. 'She's two sizes smaller than you.'

✳ ✳ ✳ • ✳ ✳ ✳ • ✳ ✳ ✳

Kitty was angry when Joe opened the front door one night, staggered over the step, tripped on the hall mat and fell on the floor at her feet in a drunken mess.

'I've had enough of this!' she screamed. 'Why do you always have to keep on coming home from that pub half drunk?'

'I always run out of money,' mumbled Joe.

McGinty used to go everywhere on his donkey. One day he went to his local pub for a shandy. When he came out, his donkey had been covered in green paint. McGinty stormed back into the pub.

'Which one of you eejits has painted my donkey green?'

Big Mick stood up. Now Mick was big and tough, the sort of guy who made King Kong look skinny.

'I did!' bellowed Big Mick. 'What about it?'

McGinty was petrified and looked up at Big Mick.

'Well I thought you'd like to know that the first coat is dry.'

~~~~~~~~~~~~~~~~~~~~~~~~~~~~~~~~~~~~~~~

Paddy wanted to prove that not all Irishmen were thick. He went up to a shepherd in a field full of sheep and put on an English accent.

'Ere mate, if I can guess the exact number of sheep what you have in this field, can I take one home?'

The shepherd agreed.

'OK,' said Paddy, 'let's have a look. Right! There's 347 sheep in this field.'

'That's right,' said the shepherd.

'And now if you don't mind, mate, I'll have one of your sheep.'

'You're Irish aren't you?'

'How can you tell?' asked Paddy surprised.

'Could I have my dog back?'

An Irishwoman was having her hair cut and after the hairdresser finished she was handed a mirror.

'Have a look and let me know what you think?' said the hairdresser.

The Irishwoman looked.

'It's very nice, but do you think I could have it a bit longer at the back?'

A scientist had made a lie detector chair. He designed it so that whoever sat it in would receive an electric shock if they told a lie. He took it to a little village to show it off.

'Who would like to try it?' he asked the assembled crowd.

'I will!' said an Irishman.

The scientist helped the Irishman to try the chair out for size. 'What do you think?'

The Irishman said, 'Well, I think...' And the chair gave him an electric shock.

Dr Mick E. Taker wasn't Ireland's greatest surgeon.

'Mr Devine, I've got some good news and some bad news for you.'

'What's the bad news, Doc?' asked Mr Devine.

'As you know, you were to have a leg amputated. Well, I'm afraid I cut off the wrong leg.'

'Oh dear,' said Mr Devine. 'So what's the good news?'

Dr Taker smiled.

'Your bad leg is getting better.'

A fancy dress party was in full swing when there was a knock at the door. The host opened it and there was an Irishman with a girl on his back.

'What have you come as?' asked the host.

'A tortoise,' replied the Irishman.

'But why have you got that girl on your back?'

'That's Michelle,' smiled the Irishman.

✻ ✻ ✻ • ✻ ✻ ✻ • ✻ ✻ ✻

'So what was the result of the big match you went to see?' Dawn asked Shaun.

'It was nil–nil,' Shaun told her.

'Oh?' said Dawn. 'What was the score at half time?'

'I don't know,' replied Shaun. 'The bus was late, so I missed the first half.'

✻ ✻ ✻ • ✻ ✻ ✻ • ✻ ✻ ✻

An Irishman went into his local DIY shop to return a chainsaw he had recently bought.

'What's the matter with it?' asked the assistant.

'It's not very good,' said the Irishman. 'I had a job clearing some trees and this thing was useless. I only chopped two trees down all day.'

'Let's have a look at it then,' said the assistant taking the chainsaw and pulling the cord so it screamed into life.

The Irishman jumped out of his skin.

'What's that noise?'

Now I'm not saying that he was the laziest Irishman in the Ireland, but he was the only person I knew who would flush bread down the toilet to feed the seagulls at the seaside.

❋ ＊ ❋ • ❋ ＊ ❋ • ❋ ＊ ❋

An Irishman stood up in the bar and started to sing:
'I'm proud to be an Irishman,
I'm proud to be an Irishman,
I'm proud to be an Irishman,
I'm proud to be an I... R...
I... er... S... erm...?
Oh I'm proud to be an Irishman!'

❋ ＊ ❋ • ❋ ＊ ❋ • ❋ ＊ ❋

An Irish girl goes to the doctor and tells him that her body hurts wherever she touches it.

The doctor is puzzled and asks her to show him. The Irish girl touches her knee and screams in pain. She touches her head and screams in pain. In fact whatever part of her body she touches, she screams.

'I can see the problem,' said the doctor.

'What is it?' the Irish girl asks nervously.

'Have I got a terminal illness?'

'Oh no,' reassures the doctor, 'but you have broken your finger.'

An Irish wolf was prowling through the forest looking for food. Suddenly there was a loud snap! followed by a yelp, as the wolf got caught in a bear trap. In desperation to escape, the wolf chewed off three of its legs, but was still stuck.

An Irishman was on the *Antiques Roadshow* and one of the experts was looking at what he had brought in.

'And you say you found this in your loft?' said the expert.

'That's right Sir,' the Irishman replied. 'It's been up there for years.'

The expert shook his head. 'Well I'm afraid that it isn't worth a penny.'

'Why's that?' asked the Irishman.

'It's your water tank.'

'Hey Boylan,' called Moylan over the garden fence one summer's afternoon. 'Are you using your lawn mower today?'

'Yeah,' replied Boylan.

'Great!' said Moylan. 'Then can I borrow your golf clubs? You won't need them as you're going to be busy.'

At a school assembly, a doctor was giving a lecture on the evils of drink. He put two glasses on the table in front of him and a big fat worm in each. He poured water into one glass and Irish whiskey into the other. The worm in the glass of water bobbed about happily, but the worm in the whiskey died immediately.

'So what does this little demonstration prove to you all?' asked the doctor.

O'Malley called from the back of the room:

'If you suffer from worms, drink a lot of whiskey.'

Two Irishmen had spent a successful day fishing from a boat. Just before they set off for shore, one of them painted a cross on the side of the boat.

'What you doing?' asked the second Irishman.

'By doing this, next time we can come back to the same spot to fish.'

'Oh you are an eejit,' said the second Irishman. 'We might not get the same boat again.'

A little Irish girl was talking to her little sister.

'You know Father Christmas?' said the litte Irish girl.

'Yes,' answered her little sister.

'Well, I think it's Daddy.'

'Why?'

'Because he never shaves and only works one day a year.'

An Irishman had bought his first-ever video player and so he went down to the video shop and hired out *Gladiator*. Unfortunately when he got it home and put it in his player he couldn't see anything. He phoned up the video shop and explained his problem. The clerk was very helpful.

'Is your television tuned into the right channel?' he asked.

'What television?'

It was lunchtime and an Irishman was sitting high up in the scaffolding with his lunchbox.

'Oh not cheese sandwiches again. I hate them,' he said to his mate.

The next day the same thing. This went on all through the week, and on Thursday the Irishman said to his mate, 'If I get cheese sandwiches tomorrow, I'm going to throw myself off this scaffolding.'

Come Friday, the Irishman opens his lunchbox, sees the cheese sandwiches and promptly throws himself off the scaffolding.

The Foreman and the Irishman's mate stand round the splattered body and the Foreman says, 'It's such a shame, all this over cheese sandwiches.'

'I know, and he always used to make his own.'

Two Irish pilots had just landed their plane for the first time at Shannon Airport.

'That was a good landing,' said the first pilot, 'considering how short this runway is.'

'I know, and would you look how wide it is?' said the co-pilot.

❋ ✳ ❋ • ❋ ✳ ❋ • ❋ ✳ ❋

An Irishman was working so hard on the building site, carrying a massive hod load of bricks up and down a ladder that it was beginning to worry his friend.

'Hey,' said the friend, 'don't work too hard! It doesn't look good for the rest of us if the Site Foreman sees.'

'Oh don't panic about that,' said the Irishman. 'I've got him fooled. It's the same load of bricks each time.'

❋ ✳ ❋ • ❋ ✳ ❋ • ❋ ✳ ❋

'Doc, I feel really strange,' an Irishman told his doctor. 'I keep feeling that I can see into the future.'

'That's very interesting,' said the doctor. 'When did these strange feelings start?'

'Next Thursday.'

An Irishman was in a restaurant and had called the waiter over.

'Excuse me,' he said. 'The peas with this meal are disgusting. They're hard as rocks.'

The waiter picked up a spare fork and scooped up some peas from the Irishman's plate, put them in his mouth and ate them.

'They seem perfectly soft to me,' said the waiter snootily.

'Well they would be,' replied the Irishman. 'I've been chewing them for the last half hour.'

~~~~~~~~~~~~~~~~~~~~~~~

A little Irish boy came home from school early one day because the boy next to him in class had been smoking. His mum was livid and rang up the school to complain.

'Why is it,' she raged down the phone, 'that my son gets sent home because the boy next to him is smoking? It's disgraceful.'

'But Mrs O'Donnell,' said the head teacher. 'It was your son who set him on fire!'

A group of Irish school kids were on a ferry going to France. Their teacher went through the safety drills.

'OK class, let's just check what we do in emergency. If one of you falls overboard, what do the others shout?'

'Child overboard!' they all shouted in unison.

'That's right,' smiled the teacher. 'And what would you shout if a teacher fell overboard?'

Little Kenny put up his hand.

'Excuse Miss, which one?'

A pilot was flying in a hot air balloon and was lost somewhere over Limerick. He looked down and saw a farmer out in a field and shouted down.

'Hello there, where am I?'

The Irish farmer looked up.

'Oh you can't fool me, you're in that little basket.'

An Irishman's house was ablaze and he rang the fire brigade up in a panic.

'Me house is on fire, me house is on fire. Help me!' he screamed down the phone.

'Don't panic, Sir,' said the operator. 'We will be on our way. We just need to know how we can get to your house?'

'Well I suggest that big red truck with the flashing blue light,' replied the Irishman.

An American tourist arrived in Wicklow and asked a local to show him the biggest building in the town.

'There you are,' said the local pointing to a large house. 'The biggest house in Wicklow.'

The American looked at the house and laughed. 'You call that a building, Buddy? Back home we have buildings ten times the size of that.'

'That I don't doubt!' The local smiled. 'That's the local lunatic asylum.'

✸ ✶ ✸ • ✸ ✶ ✸ • ✸ ✶ ✸

An Irishman went to see his doctor.

'What is it?'

'It's me right arm, Doc,' said the Irishman. 'It aches so much.'

The doctor took a look at the Irishman's arm.

'It's old age I'm afraid.'

'Old age?' replied the Irishman. 'My left arm is the same age. How come that one doesn't ache as well?'

✸ ✶ ✸ • ✸ ✶ ✸ • ✸ ✶ ✸

Paddy had nasty accident at work and got his ear cut off and he couldn't find it. Finally Thaddy picked up the ear from behind a machine.

'Here it is, Paddy!'

Paddy looked at the severed ear. 'That's not my ear, Thaddy! Mine had a pencil behind it.'

Did you hear the one about the Irish girl who went to the Doctor's?

'Doctor, I don't know what's the matter with me recently,' she said. 'Some days I just don't know where I am, at all, at all?'

'Fares please!' shouted the bus conductor.

＊ ＊ ＊ • ＊ ＊ ＊ • ＊ ＊ ＊

An Irish mugger stopped a man in a street and said.

'Give me all your money or else.'

'Or else, what?' asked the man.

'Look, don't confuse me,' said the mugger. 'This is the first time I've done this.'

＊ ＊ ＊ • ＊ ＊ ＊ • ＊ ＊ ＊

Did you hear the one about the Irish farmer who stood out in a paddock for three days?
Apparently he wanted to win the Nobel Peace Prize and to do that he was told he had to be outstanding in his field!

＊ ＊ ＊ • ＊

An Irishman went for a job as a miner and at the interview was asked what he knew about gas regulations. The Irishman thought long and hard and then answered, 'Well I know it's mark 7 for Toad in the Hole.'

'I just had a loft extension,' boasted an Irishman.

'I bet that was expensive,' said his friend.

'It was,' answered the Irishman, 'and it really upset the man in the flat above.'

Now we're not saying that he was the smelliest man in Ireland, but one day he decided to put some 'odour-eaters' in his shoes. Five minutes later he had disappeared.

Did you hear the one about the two Irish boys who got a sledge for Christmas?

One of them used it for going down the hill and the other used it for going up!

Did you hear the one about the Irishman who fell into the grave he had just dug?

He wasn't actually a gravedigger. He was just filling in for a friend.

'Right lads,' said the building site foreman, 'one more thing before you start your first day. All you lads can have one hour for lunch and all you Irish lads have fifteen minutes for lunch.'

'Ach, that's not fair!' said one of the Irish lads. 'How comes they get an hour for lunch and we only get fifteen minutes?'

'So we don't have to keep retraining you.'

Did you hear the one about the Irishman who was sacked from the banana packing factory?
The boss said to only pack the perfect bananas so he threw away all the bent ones!

A young Irishman runs into a bar and shouts,

'Call me a doctor! Will someone please call me a doctor?'

'What's wrong?' asks the barman. 'Are you ill?'

'No,' replies the Irishman. 'I've just graduated from medical school!'

Mary was staring at Colleen as she put lipstick on her forehead.

'Colleen, what are you doing?' asked a confused Mary.

'My boyfriend is taking me out tonight and he said that I need to make my mind up.'

An Irishman was complaining to his friend about his constipation.

'It's awful,' the Irishman said. 'I can be on the loo for hours and hours.'

'Do you take anything?' asked his friend.

'Oh yeah, I always take me newspaper and maybe a book.'

Cath O'Keely went into her local James Bond-themed hairdressers called 'Dye Another Day' and talked to Maurice, the head hair-dresser.

'Maurice, I want you to make me look ten years younger.'

'I'm sorry Mrs O'Keely,' said Maurice, 'this is a hairdresser's, not a time machine.'

✳ ✳ ✳ ● ✳ ✳ ✳ ● ✳ ✳ ✳

Two Irish boys were boasting in class.

'I ran the hundred metres in five seconds,' claimed one.

'No way!' scoffed his friend. 'That's less than the world record.'

'Well,' said the first Irish boy, 'I know a short cut.'

✳ ✳ ✳ ● ✳ ✳ ✳ ● ✳ ✳ ✳

'Of course you all know why God invented whiskey?' the Irish professor asked his class.

Dillon, a bright student put up his hand and said, 'Sir, was it to prevent us Irish from ruling the world?

✳ ✳ ✳ ● ✳ ✳ ✳ ● ✳ ✳ ✳

The Irish Space programme had a press conference where they announced to the world's press that they were to send a manned spaceship to the sun.

'But you can't do that!' said one reporter. 'The sun is so hot that anyone who went anywhere near it would be burned alive.'

'Ah, but our scientists have thought of that,' said the leader of the programme smugly. 'That's why we are going at night.'

Did you hear the one about the Irishman who bought a piece of wrapping paper that was 1 inch by 30 metres so that he could send his Mammy a new washing line?
Unfortunately she sent it back because her garden wasn't long enough!

❋ ❋ ❋ • ❋ ❋ ❋ • ❋ ❋ ❋

Mary was on the phone to her friend, Betty telling her all about her new digital television.

'Oh I can't get digital television where I am,' said Betty.

'Where's that?' asked Mary.

'In the garden,' replied Betty.

❋ ❋ ❋ • ❋ ❋ ❋ • ❋ ❋ ❋

An Irishman was walking in a park and he saw another man throw a stick into a lake. The man's dog walked on the water, picked up the stick and brought it back. The man did this a couple of times while the Irishman watched in amazement.
Finally he went up to the man.

'So, when are you going to teach your dog to swim?'

A television reporter was interviewing a man for making a brave citizen's arrest.

'Well, the police couldn't do it, the Paramedics couldn't do it, and the fire brigade couldn't do it. How did you get the one-armed Irish cat burglar out of that tree?'

'Oh it was easy,' said the man. 'I just waved to him.'

~~~~~~~~~~~~~~~~~~~~~~~~

An Irishman was driving down a road, swerving all over the place. Finally the police stopped him.

'Oh thank goodness you're here,' he said to the policeman. 'I was driving down this road when all of a sudden this tree appeared in front of me. I swerved to avoid it, then another one appeared. I missed that one. Then another one appeared and another one and...'

'Sir,' said the policeman. 'May I suggest you take that pine-scented air freshener down from your mirror?'

~~~~~~~~~~~~~~~~~~~~~~~~

An Irishman was a bit the worse for drink at a party when he talked to the host.

'Excuse me, but do you know if lemons have legs and feathers?'

'Of course they don't!' said the host.

'Oh dear,' slurred the Irishman. 'I think I've just squeezed your canary into my gin and tonic.'

An Irishman walks into a pub and is surprised to see another Irishman up at the bar who he recognises.

'Terence O'Milligan,' says the Irishman. 'I haven't seen you in years. Haven't you changed? You used to be thin, but now you're fat. You used to be ginger, but now you're bald. You used to be clean-shaven, but now you've got a beard. I wouldn't have known you!'

The other Irishman looks at him in a somewhat confused state.

'My name's Michael O'Rourke.'

'Would you look at that,' exclaims the Irishman. 'You've even changed your name!'

Finnegan had died and his wife Mary invited everyone back to the house for the wake. Finnegan's brother was first back and saw that the front room was full of crates of stout, whiskey, lager, cider, beer and wine. On the table near the alcohol mountain was a plate with two slices of bread on it. When Mary entered the room Finnegan's brother asked:

'Mary, what's all the bread for?'

Three Irishmen were driving across the desert when their truck broke down.

'We're going to have to walk,' said the first one. 'We'd best take what we can from the truck to help us make it across the desert. I'll take this big bottle of water.'

'I'll take this bag of food,' said the second one.

'And I'll take this!' said the third Irishman, removing the driver's door.

'What on earth do you want to take that for?' asked the first.

'Well, when we're walking across the sand,' explained the third Irishman, 'and we get a bit hot, we could wind the window down to help cool us down.'

❋ ❋ ❋ • ❋ ❋ ❋ • ❋ ❋ ❋

An Irishman went to see Riverdance when it toured Dublin. When he arrived at the theatre the clerk in the box-office asked:

'And where would you like to sit, Sir?'

'The shallow end.'

❋ ❋ ❋ • ❋ ❋ ❋ • ❋ ❋ ❋

Two Irish girls are walking down the road when one of them notices a small compact on the pavement and picks it up. She opens it and looks into the mirror.

'I'm not sure who this belongs to, but her face looks very familiar.'

'Here, let me have a look.'

The second girl looks in the mirror. 'You eejit, it's me.'

'Oh it must be yours then!'

'It can't be!' says the second girl. 'I lost mine along this road some time last week.'

An Irishman went into a museum and accidentally knocked over a Ming vase. The museum curator went ballistic.

'Do you know that that vase you just knocked over was over a thousand years old?!' she screamed.

'Sure that oul thing,' smiled the Irishman. 'It's lucky it wasn't new.'

✳ ✳ ✳ • ✳ ✳ ✳ • ✳ ✳ ✳

A blind tourist called Seymour walks into a pub in Dublin. He orders a drink.

'Who wants to hear some Irish jokes?' he shouts. The whole pub goes quiet and then Seymour hears the barman's Irish accent.

'Before you tell any Irish jokes,' he growls, 'I think it's best to warn you that I'm Irish, and so is my barmaid, a black belt in karate. She lives with one the bouncers on the door, who is 6 foot 7, weighs 200lb and is a professional Irish wrestling champion. Also there are six big Irish rugby players sitting over in the corner. So think about this and ask yourself – do you really want to tell any Irish jokes in this pub?'

'No, not now,' says Seymour. 'Especially if I'm going to have to explain them all nine times.'

Did you hear about the fire in the Irish library?
Both the books were burnt, even the colouring-in ones!

An Irishman asked his wife what she would like for her birthday.

'Oh I'd love to be ten again!' she said wistfully.

So on her birthday before she could say anything, her husband whisked her off to a theme park. He took her on all the rides. He bought her candyfloss and afterwards took her to see a *Harry Potter* movie. After that he treated her to a burger dinner with the free toy and when they got home, he told his exhausted wife that she could stay up until nine o'clock as it was her birthday. Just before she went to bed he also made her some hot chocolate.

'Did you enjoy being 10 again?' he asked.

'I meant size 10!' his wife snapped.

The Irishman's wife watches as he swipes flies in the living room.

'Killed any yet?'

'Five!' says he proudly. 'Three males and two females.'

'How could you tell what sex they were?'

'Easy,' says the Irishman. 'Three were on a beer can and two were on the phone.'

An Irishman was showing his best friend around his new flat after a night out on the drink. His friend was curious about the big gong that stood in the middle of the living room.

'What's that?'

'It's my new speaking clock.'

'So how does it work?'

'I'll show you.'

The Irishman picked up the hammer and struck the gong with a resounding clang! Suddenly there was knocking from the other side of the wall followed by a very irate voice.

'Can you not hit that gong so loudly! Do you know it's a quarter past three in the morning!'

Mal met Cal at a local football match.

'How's the game going?'

'Great!' said Cal. 'It's end to end stuff.'

'Good match, then?'

'It is,' said Cal, 'and I think it's down to the managers and their motivational skills.'

'What do you mean?' asked Mal.

'Well the manager of the team in red has promised every man that scores a free bottle of stout. While the manager of the whites had promised every man who scores a bottle of best Irish whiskey.'

'That sounds interesting!' Mal said.

'What's the score at the moment?'

'72 all!' replied Cal.

'I put on a clean pair of pants and a clean pair of socks, every day,' an Irishman boasted to no one in particular. 'The only problem is, come the end of the month, I can't get me trousers and shoes on.'

❋ * ❋ • ❋ * ❋ • ❋ * ❋

Two Irishmen met one day.

'Hey, do you remember Ardel O'Flynn, from school?' said the first Irishman.

The second Irishman thought for a while.

'Yeah I remember O'Flynn, always came top of the class, went to Cambridge and got a doctorate in chemical engineering and a degree in medicine. He also toured the world and wrote a book, in Russian, on the political state of Eastern Europe.'

'That's the one. Well I met him the other day!'

'Really, what did you say to him?' the second Irishman asked.

'Do you want fries with that?'

❋ * ❋ • ❋ * ❋ • ❋ * ❋

Paddy and Thaddy were walking past a forest when they saw a sign that read: 'Wanted. Tree Fellers.'

'Oh that's a shame!' said Paddy. 'If Shamus had been with us, we could have applied for that job.'

The Irishman noticed that his little daughter had made a fire engine out of a pram, a garden hose and a little ladder. He also noticed that she had not only tied a rope from the toy engine to the collar of the family's pet dog, to help pull it along, but also another rope from the toy engine to the tail of the family cat.

'That's a lovely fire engine you've got there, but don't you think it would be better if you tied the rope round the cat's collar?'

'But Daddy, I wouldn't have a siren then!'

✳ ✳ ✳ • ✳ ✳ ✳ • ✳ ✳ ✳

The Dublin building site manager wasn't one of Ireland's most compassionate men. One of his scaffolders arrived an hour late for work one morning all covered in bumps, bruises and blood. The manager asked what had happened.

'I fell down the stairs!'

'And that took you a whole hour?'

✳ ✳ ✳ • ✳

'Waiter!' called the Irishman as he sat in an expensive restaurant.

'Yes Sir?' replied the waiter.

'This soup is horrible. It has no taste, it's watery and it smells of lemon.'

'That's your finger bowl, Sir,' sniffed the waiter.

An Irishman had just spent a romantic night with his new girlfriend when he noticed a picture of a man on her mantlepiece.

'That's not your husband, is it?' he asked nervously.

'No, of course not,' she said.

'Is it your boyfriend?'

'No,' said the girl. 'You're my boyfriend now.'

'Is it a relative?'

'No.'

'Well who is it then?' the Irishman demanded.

'You are silly,' said the new girlfriend. 'It's me before the surgery.'

~~~~~~~~~~~~~~~~~~~~~~~~

Two Irishmen knocked on the door of their local convent. The Mother Superior opened it and asked the Irishmen what they wanted.

'Excuse me, Mother Superior,' said one, 'but do you have any nuns here that are under three feet?'
The Mother Superior thought about it.

'No, we don't. If we did have a nun that small, I would surely know about it.'

'Oh thanks very much,' said the first Irishman in relieved tones.

'See? I told you it was a penguin we knocked down in the truck.'

Did you hear about the Irish girl who had to give up her cello lessons?

The cello was too heavy and it really hurt her neck when she put it under her chin!

The priest was giving a sermon on the evils of drink.

'…and if you continue to drink, you will gradually get smaller and smaller until you're the size of a mouse.'

When the Irishman got home he told his wife what the priest had said.

'So are you going to give up the drink?'

'No,' he replied. 'I'm going to kill the cat.'

Thaddy's wife noticed her husband leaning over the neighbour's fence. Every so often he would shout:

'Green side up!'

She watched for a while and her husband kept on shouting.

'Green side up! Green side up!'

'Thaddy,' she eventually called. 'What's going on?'

'It's Paddy, next door,' he called back. 'He's laying some new turf.'

An Irishman in America met two guys in a bar and had a few pints. One guy said that there was a building a few blocks away where, because of the strange wind thermal around it, one could jump off the building and float. The Irishman said that he didn't believe it, but the two guys said they would show him.

'Watch!' said the first guy as they stood on the roof of the building. To the Irishman's amazement, the guy leapt off the building, floated for a few seconds and then landed back on the roof.

'That's amazing. Let me have a go!' said the Irishman as he leapt into the air... and fell 50 storeys to his death.

The guy who hadn't jumped off the building turned to the guy who had.

'You know, Superman, you're quite nasty after you've had a few drinks.'

❋ * ❋ • ❋ * ❋ • ❋ * ❋

It was an Irishman's first day on the Cork building site and already things weren't going too well. The foreman really confused him – he showed him a selection of spades and told him to take his pick.

An old Irishwoman went to her local newspaper and asked the girl on the desk how much was it to put a death notice in the paper, as her husband of 45 years had recently died.

'It's a pound a word,' said the girl.

So the old Irishwoman wrote on a piece of paper "Bill is dead."

'Is that all you want?' asked the girl.

'It's all I can afford,' said the old Irishwoman.

Feeling sorry for the old woman, the girl opened her purse and gave her three pounds.

'There, you can write a bit more now.'

The old Irishwoman thanked the girl and wrote on another piece of paper.

"Bill is dead. Lawnmower for sale."

✳ ✳ ✳ • ✳ ✳ ✳ • ✳ ✳ ✳

So how many Irishmen does it take to change a light bulb?

Six – one to change the light bulb, two to get the drinks in and three to sing about how grand the old bulb was.

An Irishman was walking with his horse when a tourist rushed up to him.

'What a wonderful horse. How much?'

'I'm not selling him because he don't look too good,' said the Irishman.

'He looks wonderful!' the tourist replied.

'I'll give you £1000.'

'But he don't look too good,' repeated the Irishman.

'Rubbish, he looks great. How about £2000?' He rubbed his head. 'I'm not sure.'

'OK,' said the tourist. 'Here's £10,000. It's yours if you let me buy your horse and ride away on it.'

'OK,' said the Irishman and next minute he was £10,000 richer and the tourist had mounted the horse and galloped off... straight into a tree.

The Irishman was standing over the tourist when he came round, and said.

'You didn't tell me that your horse was blind?!'

'Well,' said the Irishman, 'I did tell you that he didn't look too good.'

An Irishman went to see his doctor.

'It's drink that's made you into the slovenly, drunken, incontinent, rude and violent person that you are.'

'Oh thanks Doc!' said the Irishman, greatly relieved. 'And the wife always said it was my fault.'

An Irishman was sitting in the lounge bar at Dublin Airport chatting to the barman.

'I've come to meet my brother,' he said.

'He's flying in from Australia and I haven't seen him for forty years.'

'That's nice,' said the barman. 'Do you think you'll recognise him after all these years?'

'Probably not,' sighed the Irishman. 'After all, he has been away for a long time.'

'He probably won't recognise you either,' smiled the barman.

'Oh, of course he will! I haven't been away at all.'

An Irishman was stuck in an Irish bog and sinking fast. Luckily his neighbour was passing by and offered to pull him out. Now although he is a strong man and the Irishman was a titchy little fella, the neighbour just couldn't pull the little Irishman out. He pulled and he heaved, but to no avail.

'I'm going into town to get some help,' said the neighbour.

'You can't do that!' screamed the Irishman. 'I'd have sunk by then.'

'Well, what else can we do?' asked the neighbour.

'You could try again and this time I'll take me feet out of the stirrups.'

A priest walks into a pub and talks to the first Scotsman he meets.

'Do you want to go to heaven?'

'I do Father,' says the man.

'Good on you. Then go stand by the wall.'

The priest then talks to an Englishman.

'Do you want to go to heaven?'

The Englishman is quick to answer.

'Certainly, Father.'

'Good on you, too. Go stand by the wall.'

Finally the priest comes up to an Irishman.

When asked the same question, the Irishman says 'No'.

'I don't believe this!' exclaims the priest. 'You're saying that when you die you don't want to go to heaven?'

'Oh, when I die, I do,' says the Irishman. 'I thought you were getting a group together to go straight away.'

A tourist walks into a cocktail bar in Dublin, looks at what is on offer, then orders an 'Irish Cocktail.' He gets a pint of stout with a potato in it!

An Irishwoman was standing by a full-length mirror in her underwear, while her husband was in bed reading.

'Oh look at me. I'm fat. I'm going grey. My backside is enormous. My bust is saggy and every day I seem to get another wrinkle. I just feel I look oul and ugly.'

'I'll tell you something though,' said her husband, lowering his book.

'What's that?' asked the Irishwoman.

'There's nothing wrong with your eyesight.'

✳ ✳ ✳ • ✳ ✳ ✳ • ✳ ✳ ✳

An Irishman was going up to the top deck of a bus when he spoke to the conductor.

'Can I bring up a crate of stout?'

The conductor thought for a bit.

'I don't see why not.'

'Thank you,' said the Irishman and promptly threw up over the stairs.

✳ ✳ ✳ • ✳

You can always spot the Irishman on the North Sea Oil Rigs. He's the one throwing bread to the helicopters.

An Irishman goes into an electrical shop and speaks to one of the assistants.

'Excuse me, where do you keep the Potato Clocks?'

'I'm sorry, Sir,' says the assistant, 'you want what?'

'I want a Potato Clock,' insists the Irishman.

'I'm afraid Sir, there is no such thing as a Potato Clock.'

'There must be!' says the Irishman. 'My boss told me yesterday that I've got to get a Potato Clock, so that I can be at work by half past eight.'

~~~~~~~~~~~~~~~~

An Irish girl was driving along the motorway when she got a call from her boyfriend.

'Be careful! I've just heard on the radio that there's a car going the wrong way down the motorway you're on.'

'It's not just one car,' said the Irish girl. 'There's hundreds of them.'

~~~~~~~~~~~~~~~~

The doctor rang up the old Irish gent to see if the pills he had prescribed a couple of weeks ago had improved his strength.

'Not very well,' wheezed the old Irish gent. 'I can't get the lid off the bottle.'

An Englishman, a Scotsman and an Irishman wanted to get in to see the Dublin Olympics, but they didn't have tickets. The Englishman saw a nearby building site and had an idea. He stripped down to his vest and shorts, grabbed a piece of scaffolding and went up to the competitors' gate.

'Smith, pole vault,' he said. The guard let him in.

The Scotsman did the same, only he picked up a sledgehammer and said, 'MacDonald, hammer thrower,' and he was let in.

The Irishman arrived at the gate covered in scratches, cuts and blood on account of the barbed wire he had wrapped around himself.

He hobbled up to the guard and said, 'O'Grady, fencing.'

While most Irish girls are very pretty, one of them certainly wasn't. When she went into a room, mice threw themselves on to traps. One day she went into the confessional box. 'Bless me, Father, for I have sinned.'

'What is it, child?' asked the priest.

'Father, I have committed the sin of vanity!' bellowed the ugly Irish girl. 'I keeping looking in the mirror at home and telling myself how beautiful I am.'

The priest turned and looked at her.

'My child, I have good news. That isn't a sin – it's a mistake.'

Two Irish hunters had gone to America to hunt bear. While they were driving through what they were told was 'Bear Country', they came to a fork in the road.

'Would you look at that!' said one of the Irishmen pointing to a road sign that read BEAR LEFT.

'We're too late.'

❋ * ❋ • ❋ * ❋ • ❋ * ❋

An Irish girl was working as a waitress in a Dublin restaurant when a fat fussy tourist called her over. He was holding up a piece of pork with a fork.

'Waitress,' he sneered, 'look at this, does it look like a pig to you.'

'Which end of the fork are we talking about, Sir?' the Irish girl sweetly smiled.

❋ * ❋ • ❋ * ❋ • ❋ * ❋

An Irishman and his wife returned home early and could hear their son in the living room about to propose to his girlfriend. The Irishman's wife didn't want to be accused of eavesdropping and spoiling the moment.

'Should we cough and let them know we can hear them?'

'Cough? Why should I cough?' said the Irishman. 'Nobody coughed to warn me when I proposed to you.'

Three Irishmen walked out of the pub one lunchtime, into a windy street.

'Bejabers, it's windy,' said one.

'No it's not!' replied the second. 'It's Thursday.'

'So am I,' said the third man. 'Let's go and have another drink.'

✳ ✳ ✳ • ✳ ✳ ✳ • ✳ ✳ ✳

Up till now Nolan and Dolan had never left their very remote village. They were taking their first-ever train ride up the west coast of Ireland. An attendant pushing a refreshment trolley arrived and asked the boys if they would like something.

'What's that bent yellow thing?' asked Nolan.

'I don't know,' said Dolan.

'It's a banana, Sir,' said the attendant.

Having never seen or tasted a banana before, the two boys bought one each. Nolan had just bit into his as the train went into a tunnel. When it emerged, Nolan threw the banana away.

'I wouldn't eat that banana if I was you,' he said to Dolan. 'I took one bite and I went blind there for a couple of seconds.'

An Irish girl saw her Dublin boss standing near the office shredder looking bemused. She asked if she could help.

'Yes,' said the Dublin boss. 'This is a very important report. Do you know how this thing works?'

The Irish girl turns on the machine, takes the report from her boss and proudly feeds it into the machine.

'Oh that's brilliant! Thank you. I just need two copies.'

Did you hear about the unlucky Irishman?

He was crossing the road when a car hit him and knocked him thirty feet in the air, over a hedge and into a field. The police charged him with leaving the scene of an accident!

Ireland was due to meet Scotland in a big international rugby match so the Manager of the Irish team decided to get in some extra training. He rang up Madam Tussaud's in London and asked if he could borrow the waxworks of the Scottish team, so that the Irish lads could practice some moves.

The waxworks were delivered to Lansdowne Road and training began. A couple of days later, an official from the Irish Rugby Board rang up to see how things were going.

'Not too good,' said the Manager. 'We had a practice match yesterday. Scotland won 16-4.'

An Irishman was walking through a back street in London when a mugger armed with a gun stepped out in front of him.

'Right, you!' he spat. 'Your money or your life?'

'You'll have to shoot me,' said the Irishman. 'I'm saving up for me old age.'

Pat was curious when he saw Mick pouring some of his best Irish whiskey onto his lawn.

'What you doing, Mick?'

'Saving time and energy,' said Mick.

Pat didn't understand.

'You know what a chore mowing the lawn is? Well, this is the best way to avoid cutting your grass. Just pour Irish whiskey on it.'

'How can that save you time and energy?' asked a still confused Pat.

'Well,' said Mick, 'the grass comes up half-cut already'.

An American went into a Dublin bar and thought he'd wind the barman up.

'Hey buddy, got any of them Helicopter Chips?'

The barman replied without a second thought.

'Sorry, Sir, we only do plain.'

Paddy rang Thaddy up to tell him about the trouble he was having with a jigsaw.

'It's very difficult,' said Paddy. 'There's loads of pieces, but I just can't seem to get them to join together and make the same picture of the tiger that's on the box.'

Thaddy told him not to worry and that he would be round soon to help.

When Thaddy arrived he saw Paddy sitting at a table trying to do his jigsaw. Thaddy looked at the pieces and looked at the box.

'Paddy, put the Frosties back in the box.'

✳ ✳ ✳ • ✳ ✳ ✳ • ✳ ✳ ✳

Did you hear about the very unsuccessful Irish firing squad that used to stand in a circle?
When they finally decided that that formation didn't work, they tried lining up one behind the other!

✳ ✳ ✳ • ✳ ✳ ✳ • ✳ ✳ ✳

An Englishman had always wanted to be an American and his doctor told him that there was an operation that he could undergo to remove 40% of his brain, which would leave him thinking and talking like an American. The man agreed. During the operation the doctor made a terrible mistake and waited until the man came round to tell him.

'Look,' he said when the man was awake, 'by accident, instead of 40% of your brain, I removed 75%.'

'Well bejabers,' said the man, 'you're not to be worrying too much about that, so you are.'

An Irish lad called Paddy and a Scots lad called Jock, were in the army and they were being made to march round the drill square in double quick time. The breathless Scot said to the Irishman.

'Aye, Paddy, I no like 'doubling'.'

'Well Jock, I'm not that keen on Edinburgh.'

✻ ✻ ✻ • ✻ ✻ ✻ • ✻ ✻ ✻

An Irishman had married into money, but the marriage wasn't a happy one.

'If it wasn't for my money, this big house and all the things inside it like the TV and cinema room, the gym, the games room, the antique furniture, the state of the art sound system and the indoor swimming pool,' his wife shouted, 'wouldn't be here!'

'If it wasn't for your money,' the Irishman shouted back, 'I wouldn't be here!'

✻ ✻ ✻ • ✻ ✻ ✻ • ✻ ✻ ✻

Two Irish friends were going camping in Africa.

'I'm taking four bottles of whiskey with us, just in case we get bitten by a snake. What are you taking?'

'Some snakes!'

An Irishman went into his local college and asked if he could enrol in a night course in Japanese. He was given a registration form to fill in.

'I hope you don't mind me asking?' said the registration clerk. 'Why on earth do you want to study Japanese? It's such a hard language to master.'

'I know,' said the Irishman. 'But me and the wife have just adopted a Japanese baby and we want to be able to understand him when he starts to talk.'

An Irishman went into a timber yard.

'I'd like some planks of wood please.'

'What size?' asked the assistant.

'4 by 2 please.'

'Fine,' replied the assistant. 'And how long do you need them?'

'Well I'm building a house,' said the Irishman, 'so I'd like to keep them if possible.'

It was late at night and an Irish couple were asleep in bed when the bedside phone rang.

'Hello?' said the sleepy husband. 'What? How would I know, I'm a bus driver, not a weather man.'

'What was that about?' asked his wife as she was woken up by her husband slamming the phone down.

'Some eejit of a fella wanted to know if the coast was clear.'

A little Irish girl was in her back garden filling in a large hole.

'What're you doing?' asked her neighbour who was watching over the garden fence.

'My pet goldfish has died, so I'm burying him.'

'Oh dear!' said the neighbour. 'But that's a very big hole for a little goldfish.'

'I know,' said the little Irish girl, 'but that's because he's inside your cat.'

The Irish lady was eating an evening meal with her husband.

'When we were first married, you always insisted on me having the biggest portions. You used to always make sure I had the biggest piece of steak. You don't do that any more. Is it because you don't love me anymore?'

'Don't be silly darling. It's just that you cook so much better than when we were first married.'

An Irishwoman was taking her first plane ride and was curious when the stewardess offered her a hard boiled sweet.

'It's to keep your ears from popping at high altitudes,' she explained nicely.

At the end of the flight as the Irishwoman was getting off, the stewardess asked her if the sweets had worked.

'Not really,' said the Irishwoman, 'they kept falling out.'

An Irishman carrying a large salmon under his arm walks into his local fish and chip shop.

'Excuse me, but do you sell fishcakes?'

'We do, but unfortunately we've run right out,' the owner apologises.

'Oh that's a shame,' says the Irishman, nodding to the salmon under his arm. 'It's his birthday today.'

❋ ❋ ❋ • ❋ ❋ ❋ • ❋ ❋ ❋

An Irishman was in the pub one night, boasting to everyone that he could name the capitals of all the world's countries. Of course no one believed him, but he insisted.

'OK brain-box, what's the capital of Venezuela?' asked the barman.

'That's easy,' said the Irishman. 'V!'

❋ ❋ ❋ • ❋ ❋ ❋ • ❋ ❋ ❋

An Irishwoman was tired of being embarrassed when her husband referred to her as 'Mother of Six'. They were at a party recently and he called in a loud voice,

'Time to go home, 'Mother of Six'!'

The Irishwoman replied in an equally loud voice, 'Coming, 'Father of Four'!'

❋ ❋ ❋ • ❋ ❋ ❋ • ❋ ❋ ❋

A man with a crocodile on a lead went into a pub in Wicklow and asked the barmaid.

'Excuse me miss, do you serve Irishmen?'

'Of course we do.'

'Great!' said the man. 'I'll have a pint, and an Irishman for my crocodile, please.'

An Irish lady went to see Dr Flynn D. Form, and told him of her problem.

'I keep thinking I'm cartoon characters,' she said. 'One day I think I'm Mickey Mouse, the next day I think I'm Donald Duck. This morning I woke up and thought I was Bambi.'

'That's very interesting,' said Dr Form, 'but nothing to worry about. You're just having some Disney spells.'

❋ ❋ ❋ • ❋ ❋ ❋ • ❋ ❋ ❋

Frank O' Funnell was an underwater engineer for the Irish Marine Company. One day he was working under the Irish Sea from a boat up on the surface, when he received a message over the radio.

'Frank,' said the voice. 'This is Finnegan on the boat. Don't bother coming up.'

'Why?' asked Frank.

'We're sinking,' said Finnegan, 'so we'll come down to you.'

❋ ❋ ❋ • ❋

Did you hear the one about the Irish photographer who kept all his broken light bulbs?
He needed them for his dark room!

An Irishman went into a dirty English pub and was surprised to see a pig on the counter.

'Excuse me Sir,' asked the Irishman, 'but why is that pig on the bar?'

'What pig, mate?' the barman belched.

The Irishman pointed to the porker draped across the counter.

'That's an air freshener.'

It was the Irishman's first day on the building site. He asked the foreman if he could hang his coat up in a nearby shed.

'That's not a shed,' said the foreman. 'That's your hod.'

An Irishman was on a skiing holiday in Switzerland. He went into a ski shop and asked the assistant,

'Tell me Sir, when I'm skiing down the hill, do I zig-zag or zag-zig?'

'I don't really know,' said the assistant. 'I'm a tobogganist.'

'Oh in that case,' said the Irishman, 'I'll have a packet of cigarettes and a box of matches, please.'

An Irishman was in East London and decided to visit a typical English nightclub. On the door, two big bouncers frisked him for weapons. When they found out he didn't have any, they gave him some.

An Irishman walked into a bar with a parrot on his head.

'Where on earth did you get that?' asked the barman.

'Well, it started off as a little wart on my bum,' replied the parrot.

Two Irishmen were out in a boat, fishing, when the boat sprung a leak.

'The boat's taking on water. What're we going to do?'

'Don't worry! I've made another hole down this end to let it out.'

Michael O'Shuaneghessymacker was Ireland's worst Grand Prix driver. In the Monte Carlo Grand Prix he made 100 pit stops – once to fill up with fuel, the other 99 times to ask for directions.

The Irish builder had spent six weeks building a 60 foot tall chimney in the middle of one of Farmer O'Toole's fields.

'There's it finished,' the Irish builder said as he showed the farmer. 'But why do you want a chimney in the middle of the field?'

'I don't!' Farmer O'Toole fumed. 'You've had the plans upside down. I wanted a well.'

Paddy didn't seem his usual self when Thaddy met him for a drink one night.

'What's up?' Thaddy asked.

'Oh I don't know,' sighed Paddy. 'I keep getting these spots before my eyes.'

'Really?' asked Thaddy. 'Have you seen a doctor?'

'No,' replied Paddy, 'only spots.'

✳ ✳ ✳ • ✳ ✳ ✳ • ✳ ✳ ✳

Did you hear the one about the Irish girl who spent all her money on a trip to Warsaw?

She wanted to be a Pole dancer!

✳ ✳ ✳ • ✳ ✳ ✳ • ✳ ✳ ✳

The widow of a rich Irish man sat expectantly in the solicitor's office for the reading of his will. The solicitor opened the letter and began to read.

'I, Patrick James Connelly being of sound mind... spent all my money before I died.'

✳ ✳ ✳ • ✳ ✳ ✳ • ✳ ✳ ✳

An Irish couple were parked in a secluded spot on Lovers' Lane.

'Do you want to get into the back seat?' he whispered in his girlfriend's ear.

'No, I want to stay in the front with you.'

An Irish girl was going to go to New York on her holidays and wanted to know how much time the journey would take.

'How long is the flight from Dublin to New York?' asked the Irish girl, when she rang the airline company.

'Just a minute,' said the operator.

'That quick?' replied the Irish girl.

❋ ❋ ❋ • ❋ ❋ ❋ • ❋ ❋ ❋

Did you hear about the Irishman who travelled all the way to Dublin to change his name to AIG 2065?
He did it just so he could have a personalised car registration number plate!

❋ ❋ ❋ • ❋ ❋ ❋ • ❋ ❋ ❋

No one is saying that she was a bit thick, but she was the only Irish woman I know who would smile during a lightning storm, convinced someone was taking her photograph.

❋ ❋ ❋ • ❋

Scientists have discovered a rare, native Irish butterfly in the Cork countryside. They know that the beautifully marked butterfly is Irish, because after a while it turns into a caterpillar.

Irish people are brilliant at languages. They can understand many tongues such as French, German, Italian, Russian and Swahili... as long as they're spoken in Irish.

A while ago there was talk of an Irish Mafia being set up in Belfast. It didn't last long because the Godfather Don O'Killarney kept making offers he couldn't remember or understand.

Irish stuntman Derval O'Knievel was badly injured a couple of weeks back when a stunt he was performing went wrong. He was trying to jump twenty-five motorbikes in a bus.

Did you hear the one about the Tug of War contest between Dublin and Cork?
It was cancelled because they couldn't find a long enough rope!

The captain of a Spanish galleon looked through his telescope.

'Pirates ahoy!' shouted the captain. 'Off the starboard side, and the captain is an Irishman.'

'Excuse me captain,' said the First Mate who was standing nearby. 'How do you know that the pirate captain is an Irishman?'

'Easy, First Mate,' answered the captain. 'He's the only pirate wearing a patch over each eye.'

~~~~~~~~~~~~~~~~~~~~~~~~~~~~~~~~~~

One night an Irishman brought home a pig from the pub.

'You're not bringing that thing in this house,' screamed his wife.

'Why not?' slurred the Irishman.

'Because of the smell!' she shrieked.
The Irishman burped.

'Oh don't worry about that, I'm sure he'll get used to it after a while.'

~~~~~~~~~~~~~~~~~~~~~~~~~~~~~~~~~~

Of course you all know why Irishmen go around it threes? You don't?
Well let me explain – it's because one of them can usually read, one can usually write and the third likes to hang about with intellectuals.

O'Knowe goes onto an Irish quiz show.

'What is fourteen plus fourteen?'

After a pause, O'Knowe says, 'Nineteen!'

The audience, made up of O'Knowe's friends and family and other Irish people, shouts out, 'Give him another chance! Give him another chance!'

The quiz-master smiles and asks another question.

'What is five plus five?'

After even longer than the last time O'Knowe says, 'Forty-six.'

The quiz-master shakes his head as the audience once again began to chant.

'Give him another chance! Give him another chance!'

Just before the quiz-master is about to ask the third question, he whispers to O'Knowe:

'The next answer is four, OK?'

The quiz-master ask him what two plus two is and quick as a shot O'Knowe says, 'FOUR!'

The audience go mad chanting:

'Give him another chance! Give him another chance!'

An Irishman was hiking across America and got a lift from an American husband and wife driving a pick-up truck. There wasn't a lot of room in the front, so the Irishman sat in the back of the truck.

While driving across a bridge, the husband lost control of the pick-up and it fell over the side of the bridge into a river. After the pick-up had sunk, the husband and wife fought their way out of the cab and surfaced. A couple of minutes later the Irishman came out of the water, gasping for air.

'Where have you been?' the wife called.

'I couldn't get the tailgate open,' spluttered the Irishman.

❋ ❋ ❋ • ❋ ❋ ❋ • ❋ ❋ ❋

Big Brenda O'Nasty goes to her doctor to find out why she is feeling so unwell.

'Your problem Miss O'Nasty, is that you are too fat,' says the doctor.
Brenda isn't impressed.

'I'd like a second opinion, if you don't mind.'

'OK,' replies the doctor, 'you're ugly as well.'

An Irish girl asked her doctor to recommend a diet.

'The most effective diet I know,' said the doctor, 'is the one where you eat anything you want for the first two days of your diet. Then skip the third day and then start again.'

The Irish girl did as the doctor had said. She went home and ate anything she wanted for the first two days, then she skipped the third day. Then she ate anything she wanted for the next two days, and then she skipped the third day after that. This went on for about three weeks and then she went back to see the doctor.

'So how's your diet going?'

'Not too bad,' said the Irish girl. 'The first two days are OK, but all that skipping on the third day really tires me out.'

~~~~~~~~~~~~~~~~~~~~~~~~~~~

A man was going to have new revolutionary brain transplant operation. The brain surgeon was showing him the brains he could choose from and how much they would cost.

'Well, here we have the brain of an Englishman and that's £1000. Then we have the brain of a Scotsman, which is £5000 and then there is the brain of an Irishman which would cost you £1,000,000.'

'Why is the Irishman's brain so expensive?' asked the man.

'Because it's hardly ever been used.'

The Irish boy had a feeling that his mother didn't like him when she used to give him his school packed lunch wrapped in a map. As if that wasn't bad enough, when he came home from school, his mother used to send him out to steal hubcaps off moving cars.

'Any last requests?' sneered the captain of the Mexican firing squad as Paddy stood against the wall. 'A blindfold? A cigarette maybe?'

'No,' said Paddy. 'I'd like to sing a song.'

'Very well, you sing your song, Irishman, then we shoot you.'

Paddy took a deep breath and began singing:

'40 million green bottles hanging on the wall, 40 million green bottles hanging on the wall...'

'I feel like being romantic tonight,' sighed the Irishwoman. 'Why don't you take me out for an expensive meal at an exclusive restaurant, where we can eat exotic food and drink vintage champagne? After that we can kiss and dance the night away. Why I might even let you drink champagne out of my shoe.'

'Now, that's a kind offer,' said her husband, 'but I don't think I could manage 8 pints of champagne in one night.'

An Irish student was telling his friend how he had password-protected his computer.

'And what's your password?'

'Well, don't tell anybody,' says the Irish student 'but it's "James Bond, Indiana Jones, Superman, Spider-man, Shrek, Harry Potter".'

'What made you choose a password like that?' his friend asked.

'Because,' said the Irish student, 'I was told that it had to have at least six characters.'

❋ ✻ ❋ • ❋ ✻ ❋ • ❋ ✻ ❋

A young Irish lad comes home from school one day and tells his Dad that he's got a part in the school play.

'That's great son,' says his Dad. 'What part are you playing?'

'I'm a husband of an Irishwoman.'

'That's no good son,' his Dad replies. 'Go back and tell your teacher you want a speaking role.'

❋ ✻ ❋ • ❋ ✻ ❋ • ❋ ✻ ❋

The Irish detective arrived home from work looking very down.

'What's the matter?' asked his wife.

'I've been kicked out of the Serious Crime Squad.'

'Why?'

'I kept laughing.'

'Do you know it takes three sheep to make a cardigan?' said the Irish girl to her friend.

'Really?' replied the second Irish girl.

'That's amazing! I didn't even know that sheep could knit.'

An Irishman had locked his keys in his car and spent hours bending and fiddling with a coat hanger just trying to get the door open so that he could let his family out.

An Irishman was playing cricket when he was given out for a very dubious LBW. On the way back to the pavilion, he went up to the man in the white coat.

'That was never LBW. I was never out. You only called it because I'm Irish and you think I'm too thick to know any better. We're not a race of idiots you know.'

'It's got nothing to do with me,' said the man. 'I'm just selling ice creams.'

An Irishman driving in his car was stopped by the police one night just outside Kilkenny.

'Excuse me, Sir,' said the policeman. 'Do you know you're driving without a rear light?'
The Irishman got out of his car, looked and then broke down into floods of tears. The policeman was obviously concerned.

'Now come on, Sir,' he said. 'It's not such a serious offence. There's no need to get that upset.'

'Isn't there?' sobbed the Irishman. 'Well, you tell me what's happened to my caravan?'

An Irishman is in a rich neighbourhood touting for work as a handyman when he approaches a big house. He knocks on the door and asks the man if he wants any jobs doing for £50? The man thinks for a while, then tells him that his porch round the side of the house needs painting. Could he do that for £50? The Irishman says he can.

The man tells the Irishman that all he needs is in the garden shed and to get on with it. In less than half an hour the Irishman is knocking on the front door again.

'Finished Sir!' he beams. 'I had enough paint to give it two coats.'

'Great,' says the man, complimenting the Irishman on his speed.

'All in a day's work, Sir,' says the Irishman. 'By the way, Sir, it's not a Porch, it's a Ferrari.'

An Irishman found a magic lamp and a genie willing to grant him three wishes. For his first wish the Irishman wished for a billion pounds in his Post Office savings account. The genie clapped his hands and the Irishman was now a billionaire.

Next the Irishman wished for a fleet of expensive cars. The genie clapped his hands and the Irishman was the proud owner of some Aston Martins, Porsches and Ferraris.

The Irishman's final wish was to be made irresistible to women. The genie clapped his hands and the Irishman changed into a box of chocolates.

Did you hear the one about the Irishman who was pleased when he got a 'Parking Fine' notice on his car window?
He thought the traffic warden was giving him a compliment!

An Irishman was accused of being the second in command of a big bank robbery.

'I wasn't second in command,' the Irishman told the judge. 'I was the mastermind.'

The Judge gave him two months for perjury.

An Irishwoman had bought a toilet brush and asked her husband to use it when he'd been to the toilet. A couple of days passed and the Irishwoman asked her husband if he had been using it.

'I have,' said the Irishman, 'but I prefer the toilet paper.'

Ireland's oldest inhabitant, Mrs Ann Chent, was celebrating her birthday and gave an interview to a local newspaper reporter.

'So why do you think you've lived to 110?'

'I guess it's because I was born such a long time ago,' said Ann.

An Irishman was being interviewed for a job on a Dublin building site.

'Can you make a decent cup of tea?' asked the foreman.

'I certainly can,' replied the Irishman.

'Good,' said the foreman. 'Can you drive a fork lift truck?'

'Why?' answered the Irishman. 'How big is the teapot?'

Did you hear about the Irishman who suggested to his mother-in-law that she take a holiday?
He told her to go to the Thousand Islands... and spend a week on each island!

English scientists had dug 50 metres underground in Kent and discovered small strips of copper. After studying the copper, they announced that the ancient Britons of 25,000 years ago had a nation-wide telephone network.

Hearing this the French decided to dig 100 metres underground in the Massif Central and found small pieces of glass. They studied the glass and announced that the ancient French of 55,000 years ago had a nation-wide fibre-optic telephone network.

The Irish then dug 200 metres down in the wilds of Killkenny and found absolutely nothing. They announced that the ancient Irish of 55,000 years ago had mobile phones.

✳ ✳ ✳ • ✳ ✳ ✳ • ✳ ✳ ✳

An Irishman went up to the ticket office at Waterloo station in London.

'I want to go to Paris.'

'Eurostar?' asked the ticket salesperson.

'Well I sing a bit, but I'm no Daniel O'Donnell.'

An Irishwoman was sitting at her husband's bedside after some major surgery and he was starting to recover from the anaesthesia. His eyes started to open, he saw her and quietly spoke.

'Oh, you're beautiful.' Then he drifted back to sleep.

Later he woke again.

'Oh, you're cute.'

'What happened to "beautiful"?' his wife smiled at him.

'The drugs are wearing off,' he replied.

'Now Paddy, be honest with me,' his wife asked. 'If you didn't know, how old would you think I am?'

Paddy looked at her for a minute.

'Well looking at your skin, I'd say twenty, your hair, nineteen and your figure, twenty-five.'

'Oh Paddy,' beamed his wife, 'you are a flatterer.'

'Hang on,' Paddy said. 'I haven't added them up yet.'

A hiker on holiday in Ireland saw a local Irishman getting into his car.

''Scuse me mate,' asked the hiker. 'Can you give me a lift?'

'Sure,' said the Irishman. 'That's a nice suit you're wearing, you're looking good. The world is yours for the taking. I like your smile...'

An Irishwoman was woken up one night by her husband, sitting at the foot of the bed crying.

'What's wrong?' she asked.

Her husband looked up at her through tear-drenched eyes.

'Remember, 25 years ago, when I got you pregnant? And your dad gave me the choice of either marrying you or going to jail?'

'Of course I remember!' replied his wife sympathetically.

'Well,' sobbed the Irishman, 'I would have been released tomorrow.'

~~~~~~~~~~~~~~~~~~~~~~

An eighty-year-old Irish woman made medical history when she gave birth to a baby girl. When she returned home her relatives came round to see her and the new arrival.

'Can we see the baby, mum?' her daughter asked.

'Not yet,' says the old lady. 'We have to wait until she cries.'

'Why?' asked her daughter.

'Because I forgot where I put her.'

An Irishman went up to customer services at his local supermarket.

'Excuse me,' he said to the lady on duty. 'I want to make a complaint. This vinegar I bought from here only this morning has got lumps in it.'

The woman looked at the bottle.

'Those are pickled onions, Sir.'

❋ ❋ ❋ • ❋ ❋ ❋ • ❋ ❋ ❋

An Irishman walks into a job centre in Dublin.

'I'd like a job please.'

'Oh you might be in luck today,' says the woman behind the counter. 'There's a model who is also a millionnairess who has just inherited a brewery who is looking for someone who can sample the beer and take her out partying most nights of the week in her Ferrari. She will pay £1000 a day and can offer 3 months holidays.'

The Irishman is amazed, but sceptical. 'You've got to be winding me up, so you have?'

'Well,' said the woman, 'you started it.'

❋ ❋ ❋ • ❋ ❋ ❋ • ❋ ❋ ❋

'I hear Shamus was thrown out of Dublin Zoo the other day,' Paddy told Pat.

'Why?'

'He was feeding the penguins.'

'That's a wee bit harsh to throw him out for just doing that, don't you think?' replied Pat.

'Not really. He was feeding them to the lions!'

Farmer O'Dingle and Farmer O' Dell were out hunting when a hang glider flew over them.

'What's that great big thing up there?' said Farmer O'Dingle.

'It looks like a giant bird. Quick, shoot it!' suggested Farmer O'Dell.

Farmer O'Dingle took aim with his shotgun and fired.

'Did you get it?' asked Farmer O'Dell.

'I don't think so,' said Farmer O'Dingle.

'But at least it's let go of the little fella it was holding.'

✻ ✻ ✻ • ✻ ✻ ✻ • ✻ ✻ ✻

An old Irishman went to see his doctor.

'Doctor every morning round about six o'clock I have to have a wee.'

'Well at your age, that's quite normal,' said the doctor.

'But Doc,' replied the old Irishman, 'I don't wake up until eight o'clock!'

✻ ✻ ✻ • ✻

An Irishman's ambition to be the first man from Ireland to sail around the world single-handed was in tatters last night, when the Ireland Yachting Association discovered he had used two hands, and disqualified him for cheating.

A tourist went into a Dublin dress shop.

'Can I try on the lovely dress you've got in the window?'

'You can if you want, madam,' the assistant said, 'but in Ireland we prefer our customers to use the changing rooms.'

The Irishman's barbecue wasn't the success he thought it would be. The chicken, steaks, sausages and burgers were cooked to perfection, but the beans kept falling through the grill!

A Welshman, a Scot and an Englishman are standing on the bank of a very wide river that they must cross when the Welshman finds a magic lamp. He rubs it and a genie pops out and gives them each a wish.

'I wish I was 10% smarter so I could get across this river.'
Suddenly the Welshman turns into a powerful French swimmer and swims the river. The Scot sees what happens and makes his wish.

'I wish I was 25% smarter so that I could get across this river.'
Suddenly the Scot turns into a German, builds a raft from trees and sails across the river. Finally, the Englishman makes his wish.

'I wish I was 50% smarter so I could get across this river.'
Suddenly the Englishman turns into an Irishman and walks across the bridge.

One night an Irishman was walking home when four muggers jumped on him. The Irishman put up a fight but the muggers got the better of him. Finally three held him down while the fourth went through his pockets. All the mugger could find was 55p.

'55p?' the mugger exclaimed. 'You put up that fight for 55p. Why bother?'

'Oh is that all you wanted?' said the Irishman. 'I thought you were after the £500 I've got hidden in my shoes.'

'Betty?' asked Tom. 'It's such a glorious day, is it not? What do you think the neighbours would say if I mowed the lawn in just my shorts?'

'Probably that I married you for your money,' sighed Betty.

An Irishman went to heaven and arrived at the Pearly Gates. St Peter checked his name on the booking-in sheet.

'It doesn't look like we've got you booked in for today. Tell me, what was your occupation when you were alive?'

'I had my own business. I was a scrap metal merchant,' the Irishman informed St Peter.

'I just need to check something,' said St Peter. 'I'll be back in a minute.' And off he went. When he returned the Irishman had gone, and so had the Pearly Gates.

Paddy was looking at Thaddy's new dog.

'Thaddy? Your dog hasn't got a tail.'

'I know,' replied Thaddy.

'Well how do you know when it's happy?' asked Paddy.

'It stops biting me,' Thaddy sighed.

Did anybody hear about the time a few years ago when in Belfast City Hall, the Irish Philharmonic Orchestra was playing 'The Bermuda Rhapsody' and the triangle player disappeared?

An Irishman had got a job on the door of a Dublin nightclub. One night a clubber came up to him and asked if he could take a pair of jump leads into the club. The Irishman thought for a while.

'Well, OK, but just don't start anything.'

'Mammy,' called the little Irish girl as she came running in to the kitchen. 'There's a man with a bill at the front door.'

'Don't be silly,' said her Mammy. 'It must be a duck with a hat on.'

'I've been married for thirty years,' an Irishman told his pal, 'and do you know, I'm still in love with the same woman.'

'That's nice,' said his pal.

'I know, but if me wife finds out, I'm in trouble.'

❋ ❋ ❋ • ❋ ❋ ❋ • ❋ ❋ ❋

'Have we any news on that Irish woman they found drowned in her shower?' asked the detective.

'Yes Sir,' said the sergeant. 'She died through washing her hair continuously for a week.'
The detective was amazed.

'Apparently she was just following instructions,' the sergeant replied, handing the detective the empty shampoo bottle on which was written:

1. Wet hair

2. Apply shampoo

3. Wait 3 minutes

4. Rinse

5. Repeat

An Irishman brought a piece of M.F.I. self-assembly furniture and he had it constructed and ready in a matter of minutes. It wasn't difficult. The diagrams were easy to follow and the final cabinet looked just like it did in the big picture on the front of the box. It was so simple to do, a child could do it; which just goes to prove that M.F.I. stands for 'Made For Irishmen!'

An Irish boy went up to the ice cream van. 'Would you like a flake in that?' asked the ice cream man.

'Yes please!' smiled the Irish boy.

'Would you like hundreds and thousands?' the ice cream man asked again.

'No, just the one please,' said the Irish boy. 'Me mammy doesn't like me to have too much chocolate.'

'My wife told me last night that she suffers from Marital Thrombosis!' Dan told Van.

'Marital Thrombosis?' repeated Van. 'What's that?'

'I'm not sure,' said Dan, 'but the wife said she's got it because she married a clot.'

A boy had been 'chatting up' a lovely Irish lass all evening at the nightclub. It was going so well until he asked if he could see her home and she showed him a photo of her parents' house.

Did you hear about the Irishman who went to Amsterdam?
He stood outside all night waiting for the Red Lights to change!

A young Irish lass went to a hairdresser's one day, listening to a mp3 player through a set of headphones. She told the hairdresser what she wanted, but also mentioned that her headphones must not be removed. The hairdresser tried her best, but while she was brushing the lass's hair, she accidentally knocked the headphones off. Almost immediately the Irish lass went blue, collapsed and fell on the floor. The hairdresser was both shocked and very confused. She picked up the headphones and was about to put them back on when she could hear something coming from them, that wasn't music. She held the headphones closer to her ear and heard:
   'Breathe in... Breathe out...
   Breathe in... Breathe out...'

Did you hear about the Irish girl who spent a whole day in her local library?
She was studying for a blood test!

'Paddy,' called his mammy, 'why haven't you changed the water in the goldfish tank?'

'Because,' replied Paddy, 'they haven't finished drinking what they got last week.'

Two Irishmen were walking along a road.

'Hey look at that dead bird.'

The second Irishman looked up in the sky.

'Where?'

'Well what do you think of it?' asked the Englishman, who was showing Stonehenge to his Irish visitor.

'It'll be nice when it's finished,' said the Irishman.

Did you hear about the Irish woman who told her husband she would like to celebrate her birthday in something long and flowing?

He threw her in the river!

I'm not saying that he was the laziest man in Ireland, but he spent three weeks off work with a broken thermos flask.

I'm not saying that O'Flynn was lazy, but it had been such a long time since he last cut the grass in his back garden, his wife had to hang her washing out on horseback.

❋ ❋ ❋ • ❋ ❋ ❋ • ❋ ❋ ❋

Did you hear the story about the Irish snob?
She refused to travel in the same car as her chauffeur!

❋ ❋ ❋ • ❋ ❋ ❋ • ❋ ❋ ❋

Did you hear the one about the thin Irishman?
He was so thin that when he walked past the snooker table, somebody tried to chalk his head!

❋ ❋ ❋ • ❋ ❋ ❋ • ❋ ❋ ❋

An Irishman rang up his local council to complain about the big puddle he had in his back garden and asked them to do something about it. A day later they sent him three ducks.

❋ ❋ ❋ • ❋

Did you hear the one about the Irish scientist working for the fashion industry who crossed a mink with a gorilla?
He got a beautiful fur coat but the arms were too long!

An Irishman phoned the doctor.

'Doc, I need some more of those sleeping pills for my wife.'

'Why, has she run out of them?' asked the doctor.

'No,' said the Irishman, 'she's woken up!'

An Irishman went into a pub.

'A pint of less, please.'

'What's Less?' asked a puzzled barman.

'No idea,' replied the Irishman. 'But my doctor says I've got to start drinking it.'

An Irishman goes into a flag shop in Dublin and asks,

'What colour are your Irish flags?'

'Green, White and Orange,' says the shopkeeper, surprised.

'Ok' says the Irishman. 'I'll have a green one please.'

An Irishman went into a bar and ordered 4 bitters, two red wines, one white wine, two whiskeys, a gin and tonic, a coke and four packets of cheese and onion crisps.

The barman made up the order.

'Do you want a tray?'

'No thanks,' said the Irishman. 'I've got enough to carry as it is.'

An Irishman was moaning about the amount of overtime he has to work, to his wife one evening.

'Sure I'll be coming in so late one night, I'll meet myself going out to work.'

An Irishman went to his doctor.

'Doc, I've go' a problem. I ca' pro'ou'ce my Ts, my Fs and my Ns.'

'Well you can't say fairer than that then,' replied the doctor.

'Two pints of beer and an orange please,' asked the Irishman up at the bar.

'Still orange?' enquired the barman.

'Oh yes,' said the Irishman.

'She hasn't changed her mind.'

'Where's the telly gone?' called the Irishman when he walked into the pub.

'Someone broke in last night and stole it,' the landlord told him.

'Well I'm not that surprised,' said the Irishman. 'You did stick it in the corner where everyone could see it.'

Two Irishmen were walking home along some railway tracks.

'There's an awful a lot of steps here.'

'You're telling me,' said second Irishman.

'But I'll tell you what's worse; this handrail is very low.'

An Irishwoman goes to see her doctor.

'Doctor, my husband keeps washing his car.'

'That's not unusual. Most men wash their cars,' said the doctor.

'In the bath?' she sighed.

'Hey Paddy!' called Thaddy from across the garden fence. 'Are you going fishing, today?'

'Yes I am!' replied Paddy.

'Have you got worms?' asked Thaddy.

'Yeah,' answered Paddy, 'but the doctor said I could still go fishing.'

'So how's the new job?' an Irish grandpa asked his grandson.

'I'm a Monback,' replied the young man.

The grandpa looked confused. 'A Monback? What's a Monback?'

'I work in a delivery warehouse, and when the lorries arrive, I stand behind them calling, "Monback!"'

An Irish inventor has come up with shovels with padded handgrips. It's not to stop Irish builders from getting blisters on their hands – it's to make the shovel more comfortable to lean on!

Did you hear about the Irishman who was so safety-conscious that he always wore white to make sure he was seen?
Unfortunately he went out one night when it was snowing and got knocked over by a snowplough!

'Paddy, did you forget to close the lion cage door last night?' shouted the circus owner when he found that 'King' the lion had gone.

'That I did, Sir,' said Paddy. 'But I thought it wouldn't matter too much. I mean who would want to steal a lion?'

Did you hear about the Irish mother who sent her son (who was in boarding school) three socks at a time instead of two?
She did it because in his last letter home, he had said that he'd grown another foot!

'Well I've stopped my Irish setter digging up the garden,' Liam told Shaun.

'How?' asked Shaun.

'I hid the shovel.'

'I hear Ol' Finbar had a heart attack and died outside a pub last night,' Pat told Paddy.

'Was he coming out or going in?' asked Paddy.

'Going in,' replied Pat.

'Oh what a shame,' said Paddy.

An Irishman was appalled when he saw his son jumping up and down on a hedgehog.

'Son!' he called. 'What on earth are you doing there?'

'Trying to get the conker out!' his son shouted back.

'Do you know I think I've got an elephant hiding underneath my bed,' Shaun told Don when they met.

'What makes you think that?' asked Don.

'Well,' said Shaun, 'when I get into bed, my nose touches the ceiling.'

An Irishman's phone was ringing, so he picked up.

'Hello, who's speaking, please?'

There was another Irish voice on the other end of the line.

'You are.'

An Irish lass asked her Gym instructor if he could teach her to do the splits.

'I can,' said the instructor, 'but I need to know how flexible you are?'

The Irish lass thought for a moment.

'I can do Mondays and Wednesdays, but I'm busy on Tuesdays.'

An Irishman was doing a crossword but was stuck on one clue, so he rang up another Irishman to see if he could help.

'What's the clue?' asked the second Irishman.

'To egg on,' replied the first Irishman.

The second Irishman thought for a while.

'Try, "Toast".'

An Irish policeman pulled O'Riley's car over and told him that he had been driving at 50mph in a 30mph speed limit.

'I was only going 30!' O'Riley protested.

'Not according to my speedgun,' the policeman replied.

'I was only going at 30!' O'Riley shouted.

The Irish policeman was starting to get annoyed. 'Look Sir, you were doing 20 miles per hour over the speed limit.'

'It's no good officer,' said Mrs O'Riley from the passenger seat. 'He won't listen. He's always like this when he's been drinking.'

There's a knock on an Irishman's door and he opens it to see a very distressed-looking driver.

'I'm very sorry,' says the driver, 'but I think I've just run over your cat. I'm very sorry and I'll be more than happy to replace it.'

'Fine,' said the Irishman. 'What are you like at catching mice?'

A teacher was giving an English lesson to her class and was working on opposites.

'So what's the opposite of "Joy"?'

Claudia, a little English girl, puts up her hand.

'Is it "Sadness", Miss?'

'Well done Claudia!' says the teacher. 'Now who can tell me the opposite of "Anger"?'

Megan, a little Welsh girl, puts up her hand.

'Is it "Happiness", Miss?'

'Well done Megan!' says the teacher. 'Now who can tell me the opposite of "Woe"?'

Colleen, a little Irish girl, puts her hand up.

'Is it "Giddy Up", Miss?'

✳ ✳ ✳ • ✳ ✳ ✳ • ✳ ✳ ✳

An Irishman goes to the doctor with a carrot in his ear and two chips up his nose.

'Doctor,' he says. 'I'm not feeling too good.'

'I'm not surprised,' said the doctor, 'you're not eating properly.'

An Irishman meets a leprechaun who tells him that he can have one wish.

'But remember,' says the leprechaun. 'Whatever you wish for an American will get double.'

'OK!' says the Irishman. 'Give me a million pounds and then beat me half to death.'

~~~~~~~~~~~~~~~~

Three Irishmen were talking in the pub one night about the amount of control they have over their wives.

'I'll tell you what,' said one, 'just last night my wife came to me on her hands and knees.'

'Really!' said the second.

'What happened then?' asked the equally amazed third Irishman.

'She looked at me and said, "Get out from under the bed and fight like a man!"'

~~~~~~~~~~~~~~~~

'So tell me about your new diet?' Nolleen asked Colleen as they sipped wine in the new film-themed wine bar Planet of the Grapes.

'Well, all I'm allowed to eat are coconuts and bananas.'

'Is that all?' asked Nolleen. 'And have you lost any weight?'

'No really,' replied Colleen, 'but you should see the way I can climb trees these days.'

An Irish girl really liked her new fridge with all its gadgets such as the computer-controlled temperature, the automatic defrosting cycle and the self-cleaning shelves. The only thing she didn't like about it was that she still had to cut the ice up into little cubes so they would fit in the trays.

An Irishman was driving from Galway to Dublin and his wife moaned at him all the way.

She moaned at him when they set off, she moaned at him when they stopped half way, she moaned at him when they got to Dublin.

She even moaned when he untied her from the roof rack.

An Irishman took his PC to be repaired and went to collect it.

'Have you been sending e-mails?' asked the engineer.

'Yes I have,' said the Irishman. 'How did you know?'

'I found an envelope in the CD Drive.'

Did you hear the one about the Irishman who went to PC World?
He was really disappointed when he found out that it wasn't a police theme park!

❋ ❋ ❋ • ❋ ❋ ❋ • ❋ ❋ ❋

An Irish lad had met a lovely Irish lass in a nightclub and walked her home. They stood outside the door to her house.

'Thanks for a wonderful evening. Do you know you are the most wonderful girl I have ever met. You are beautiful, intelligent and funny, you don't drink, don't smoke, don't do drugs and you've just won the lotto.'

The lass smiled. 'Thank you. I'm also a very passionate woman, would you like to come in?'

The Irish lad couldn't believe his luck as the girl open the door. As he walked in to the hallway he saw a dead horse lying on the stairs.

'What's that?' he screamed.

'I never said I was tidy, did I?'

❋ ❋ ❋ • ❋ ❋ ❋ • ❋ ❋ ❋

'I think the secret to our long marriage is because we take time to go out twice a week,' an Irishman told the newlyweds at their reception. 'It's generally a restaurant. You know, a candle-lit dinner, some good wine, some soft music and some romantic dancing.'

'That's lovely,' said the bride. 'And you do that twice a week?'

'Yes,' said the Irishman. 'She goes out on Mondays, I go out on Fridays.'

Why are tourists in Ireland like clouds?
Eventually they'll go away and you'll have a really lovely day!

❋ ❋ ❋ • ❋ ❋ ❋ • ❋ ❋ ❋

An Irishwoman went to her local hospital with two very badly burned feet.

'How did that happen?' asked the nurse.

'I was making Tinned Treacle Pudding,' said the Irishwoman.

'But how did you burn your feet doing that?'

'I was only doing what it said on the tin,' replied the Irishwoman. 'It said "after opening the tin, stand in boiling water for twenty minutes".'

❋ ❋ ❋ • ❋ ❋ ❋ • ❋ ❋ ❋

An Irishman books into a hotel and the porter offers to take his bags to his room. As the door closes, the Irishman looks around and starts complaining.

'Oh no, this room won't do. This isn't a double room. Where's the en-suite bathroom and the French windows and the balcony? No, this room is rubbish, I want to change it immediately.'

'This isn't your room, Sir,' said the porter. 'It's the lift.'

It was an Irishman's first day as a news reporter and the editor of the paper asked him a question.

'So, did you go and check out that story about the woman who could sing soprano and alto at the same time?'

'I did, Sir,' said the Irishman, 'but there was no story there. The woman just had two heads.'

An Irishman went for a job on a building site.

'So, what can you do?' asked the foreman.

'I can do brick laying, plumbing, electrics, plastering, wood work, metal work, roofing, landscaping, scaffolding, in fact anything really.'

'Oh quite a little "Bob the Builder" aren't we?' said the foreman sarcastically. 'Reckon you can do anything?'

'Yes Sir!' said the Irishman.

'Can you fetch a wheelbarrow full of wind?' the foreman asked patronisingly.

'Yes,' smiled the Irishman, 'if you fill it first.'

An Irishwoman goes into a big department store in Dublin and approaches the assistant at the haberdashery counter.

'I'd like some fur gloves, please.'

'Certainly madam,' says the assistant.

'What fur?

'To keep my hands warm of course.'

Farmer O'Dell questioned one of his Irish farmhands.

'Have you ploughed that field yet?'

'I sort of have and I've sort of not?' said the farmhand.

Farmer O'Dell was confused.

'What do you mean?'

'Well I've been thinking about it.'

'So have you ploughed the field or not?' fumed the farmer.

'No,' said the farmhand, 'but I've turned it over in my mind.'

An Irishman came home very excited.

'I've got a job!' he smiled.

'Oh well done!' said his wife. 'What is it?'

'It's a leading position within the circus.'

'A leading position. That's wonderful darling,' beamed the Irishman's wife. 'So what does that entail?'

'The elephants follow me into the ring at every show.'

After an extraordinary raid on a famous Dublin jewellers, the police questioned an Irishman who had witnessed the smash and grab.

'So just let me get this right,' said the policeman. 'You saw an elephant get out of a large van, run up to the jewellers' window and kick it in with his foot? You then saw him scoop up all the jewellery with his trunk, get back in the van and drive off?'

'That's right, Sir,' said the Irishman.

'Now tell me,' asked the policeman. 'Was it an Indian or an African elephant?'

'I don't know,' answered the Irishman. 'He had a stocking over his head.'

❋ ✳ ❋ • ❋ ✳ ❋ • ❋ ✳ ❋

A man went into his local DIY shop and bought some wallpaper. At the checkout he asked the cashier, a young Irish lass:

'Can I stick the wallpaper on myself?'

'You can,' said the cashier, 'but it would look much better on the wall.'

❋ ✳ ❋ • ❋ ✳ ❋ • ❋ ✳ ❋

An Irish mother was telling her teenage daughter her five secrets to a perfect relationship.

'One: find a man who helps around the house, who cooks and cleans and has a good job; Two: find a man who can make you laugh; Three: find a man who you can trust and you know will not lie to you; Four: find a man who knows how to give you a good time.

'And finally,' says the Irish mother. 'Five: never let these four men meet each other.'

Did you hear about the recent World Tug of War Championships held in Japan?
The Irish team were disqualified for pushing!

❋ ❋ ❋ • ❋ ❋ ❋ • ❋ ❋ ❋

An Irishman goes to the doctor.

'Doc I keep singing 'Delilah', 'What's New Pussycat?' and 'The Green, Green, Grass of Home'.'

'Don't worry' said the doctor, 'you've got Tom Jones Syndrome.'

'Is that a common thing?' asks the Irishman.

"It's Not Unusual',' replied the doctor.

❋ ❋ ❋ • ❋ ❋ ❋ • ❋ ❋ ❋

A one-eyed Irishman went into a Cork cinema.

'As I've only got one eye, do you think I could get in half price?'

'Certainly not!' said the colleen in the box office. 'In fact I should charge you double.'

'Why?' asked the Irishman.

'Because with only one eye, it'll take you twice as long to watch the whole film.'

An Irishman went into a supermarket, and was paying at the checkout. The pretty Irish girl looked at his shopping, which was made up of a tube of toothpaste, a can of beer, a meal for one, and a bag of crisps.

'You're single aren't you?' smiled the Irish girl.

'You can tell that by my shopping I suppose,' said the Irishman.

'No,' said the Irish girl, 'it's because you're so ugly.'

Once upon a time an Irish brain cell ended up in an Englishman's head. The brain cell looked around, but couldn't see any other brain cells. In fact the head was empty. The Irish brain cell was getting a little scared so it called out.

'Hello, is anybody there?'

Then it heard a voice from far, far below it.

'Hello, we're down here...'

A little Irish girl came into the living room.

'Mammy we can go to bed now, Daddy's locked up for the night.'

The little Irish girl's mammy smiled. 'I don't think so poppet, Daddy isn't home yet.'

'I know,' said the little Irish girl, 'but the police have just rung to say that Daddy's locked up for the night.'

An Irishwoman watched as her husband's coffin was lowered into the ground and sobbed on a relative's shoulder.

'Oh I really blame myself for his death.'

'Oh come on,' comforted the relative. 'Why on earth would you think that?'

'Because I shot him!' wept the Irishwoman.

An old Irishman was lying on his deathbed when he could smell his wife's cooking. He opened his eyes and called for his wife, who rushed to his side.

'What are you cooking?' he asked.

'A cake,' said his wife.

'Well, you know I'm not long for this world now, but before I go could I have one last taste of your cooking?'

'What would you like?' asked his wife.

'What about some of that cake? It smells wonderful.'

'Oh you can't have that,' said his wife. 'That's for the funeral.'

An Irishman is walking down the street and about ten feet away he sees a banana skin on the pavement.

'Oh no,' he groans. 'Here we go again.'

A tourist was fishing in an Irish river when an Irishman came up and started watching him. He didn't speak to or bother the tourist or say a word at all. He just watched. Three hours passed.

'You've been standing there all afternoon watching me. Why don't you have a go at fishing yourself?'

'No thanks,' said the Irishman. 'I haven't got the patience.'

❋ * ❋ • ❋ * ❋ • ❋ * ❋

Farmer O'Dell spoke to one of his farmhands, 'Did you count the pigs this morning?'

'I did Sir,' said the farmhand. 'I counted 24.'

'24?' Farmer O'Dell said. 'There's supposed to be 25.'

'Ah now, that must have been the little blighter I saw run off before I'd finished counting.'

❋ * ❋ • ❋ * ❋ • ❋ * ❋

An Irishman was taking part in a pub quiz and it was his question.

'OK,' said the Question master. 'This is a question in three parts. Part one; who succeeded Henry the eighth?'

'Edward the sixth,' said the Irishman.

'Correct. Part two of the question: Who reigned after Edward the sixth?'

'Mary,' replied the Irishman.

'Correct again,' said the Question master.

'Here is the final part: Who followed Mary?'

'Her little lamb!'

'Bonjour!' said the Frenchman to the Irishman, who asked, 'What does that mean?'

'In France it means "Good Day".'

'Oh right,' said the Irishman. 'Well, Hot Cross Buns.'

'What does that mean?" asked the Frenchman.

'In Ireland it means "Good Friday".'

✳ ✳ ✳ • ✳ ✳ ✳ • ✳ ✳ ✳

Two old Irishmen, Clancy and Delaney shared an ancient two-roomed farmhouse somewhere way down west. When Clancy went to see relatives they asked him how things were going.

'Oh Delaney is very difficult to live with. He keeps sheep in the kitchen, goats in the bedroom and pigs in the bathroom. The smell is awful.'

'Why don't you open a window?' said the relative.

'What and let all my pigeons escape?' snapped Clancy.

✳ ✳ ✳ • ✳

Farmer O'Dingle is leaning on his gate when a man walks up to him.

'Excuse me,' says the man. 'Could you tell me the quickest way to Dublin?'

'Are you walking or driving?' asks the farmer.

'Driving,' answered the man.

'Well I'd say that that was the quickest way.'

An Irishman and a monkey were to be the only life forms on the first ever Space Shuttle to Mars. On entering the shuttle they found two envelopes marked "Monkey" and "Irishman." The monkey opened his envelope – a letter containing complicated and precise details of not only how to pilot the shuttle, but all the aims and expectations of the voyage.

The Irishman opened his envelope. The piece of paper read: "Feed the monkey."

An Irish drunk stumbles onto the bus and sits in a seat next to a priest. Smelling his breath and seeing the state he's in, the priest says, 'Sir, do you not realise that you are on the road to perdition?'

'I am?' burps the Irishman. 'I could have sworn this was the bus for Wexford.'

An Irishman pops into his local greengrocers.

'Four pound of potatoes, please.'

The greengrocer shakes his head. 'Sorry I can't do that. It's all kilos now, I'm afraid.'

'Oh I see?' says the Irishman. 'I'll have four pound of kilos, then.'

An Irishman's dad was very ill. The doctors had done all they could for him – the priest told him that the only thing that could save him was a miracle and suggested a trip to Lourdes.

So the Irishman and all his friends had a whip round and off the Irishman and his dad went. A week later the priest met him and asked how the trip went.

'He died about an hour after we arrived,' said the Irishman.

'Oh I'm sorry,' comforted the priest. 'Perhaps it was God's way of stopping his suffering.'

'I don't think so, Father,' said the Irishman. 'I think it was more to do with the speed the cricket ball was travelling when it hit him on the head.'

~~~~~~~~~~~~~~~~~~~~~~~~

An Irishman had been going to evening classes to better himself. His wife rang the college up to see how he was doing.

'He's doing quite well; he's been making straight As,' the tutor said.

The Irishman's wife was absolutely delighted.

'That's wonderful!' she said.

'It is,' replied the teacher. 'Next week, we're going to work on his wonky Bs.'

An Englishman, a bit the worse for drink, stood up in the middle of a Dublin pub and shouted at the top of his voice.

'I was born an Englishman, I shall live my life as an Englishman and by God I shall die an Englishman.'
An Irishman shouted from the back of the bar.

'For pity's sake, man! Have you no ambition?'

❋ ❋ ❋ • ❋ ❋ ❋ • ❋ ❋ ❋

An Irish lad went up to a lovely Irish lass at a party.

'Do you know I think you're the most beautiful girl here tonight?'

'Thank you,' said the girl.

'Could I call you later?' asked the Irish lad.

'I suppose so,' mumbled the Irish lass.

'Great! What's your number?' he asked eagerly.

'It's in the phone book.'

'Right!' smiled the Irish lad. 'So, what's your name?'

'That's in the phone book as well,' said the Irish lass before she walked away.

❋ ❋ ❋ • ❋ ❋ ❋ • ❋ ❋ ❋

Milly O'Silly was a maid in a big house when the mistress called her into the lounge.

'Milly!' said the mistress as she stood by the grand piano. 'Look at this piano, it's so dirty. Why, I could write my name in the dust.'

'Oh Madam,' smiled Milly, 'that's education for you.'

An Irishman visited his doctor complaining of pains in his knees. The doctor examined him.

'You're suffering from a condition called 'Kneesitis'. I suggest you take it easy for a month, rest your knees and above all don't climb any stairs, as this will put strain on your knee joints.'

After a month the Irishman went back to the doctor and after a brief examination was told that his knees were back to normal.

'Oh that's great!' said the Irishman. 'Does that mean I can climb stairs again?'

'It certainly does,' replied the doctor.

'Thank God for that. I was getting fed up having to climb the drainpipe every time I wanted to go to the toilet.'

✳ ✳ ✳ • ✳ ✳ ✳ • ✳ ✳ ✳

Did you hear about the Irishman who bought his wife a rocket for her birthday?
She was over the moon!

An Irishman comes home late from work one night and his wife is there to greet him.

'Hi dear,' she says. 'Notice anything different about me tonight?'

'You've had your hair done.'

'No,' says his wife. 'Try again.'

'You're wearing a new dress?'

'No,' said the wife slightly disappointed.

'Try again.'

'Oh I'm too tired to play this stupid game!' snapped the Irishman. 'I give up.'

'I'm wearing a gas mask!'

Irish plumber Fixus McLeek and his mate knocked on the front door of the big house.

'Did you phone for a plumber, missus?'

'I did,' said the lady. 'But that was in January, nearly six months ago.'

'Oh sorry missus!' he apologised, then turned to his mate. 'It's the wrong house Pat; the woman we're looking for phoned in December.'

An English foreman was employing labourers, but didn't want any Irishmen. So when Paddy arrived he decided to give him a test that he wouldn't be able to complete.

'OK Paddy,' he said. 'Without using numbers, I want you to represent the number 9 on this piece of paper.'

'OK Sir,' said Paddy and proceeded to draw a trio of trees.

'What's that?' the foreman asked.

'Three trees,' said Paddy, 'and three trees make nine.'

'Oh right!' replied the foreman. 'I now want you to do the same again, but this time I want you to represent 99.'

Convinced that he had got the Irishman this time, he watched as Paddy smudged his drawing.

'What's that?' he asked again.

'Well Sir, I've made the trees dirty. As anyone can tell you, dirty tree and dirty tree and dirty tree makes 99.'

So the foreman gave the Irishman the job!

Did you hear the one about the unlucky Irishman who joined the navy to see the world?

He ended up serving on a submarine!

An Irish boxer went to see the doctor about his insomnia.

'Have you tried counting sheep?' the doctor asked.

'I have,' said the boxer, 'but whenever I get to nine, I get up.'

＊ ＊ ＊ • ＊ ＊ ＊ • ＊ ＊ ＊

An Irishman was walking his dog through the graveyard when he saw another man.

'Morning,' said the man.

'No,' said Irishman, 'just walking the dog.'

＊ ＊ ＊ • ＊ ＊ ＊ • ＊ ＊ ＊

Paddy, Mick and Shamus take an intelligence test prior to working on the building site.

'OK Paddy,' says the foreman. 'What is three times three?'

'Now, Sir, that would be four thousand and sixty two.'

'Not quite,' says the foreman. It's Mick's turn. 'What's three times three?'
Mick thinks, then says 'Friday.'

'Not even close!' replies the foreman and then finally asks Shamus. 'What's three times three?'
Shamus thinks long and hard and then says, 'Nine.'

'Correct!' exclaims the foreman. 'And how did you work that out?'

'Easy,' said Shamus. 'I just subtracted four thousand and sixty-two from Friday.'

A tourist walking through the Irish countryside stopped to ask the Irish farmer what he was building.

'Well Sir, if I can rent it out,' said the Irish farmer, 'it's a rustic Irish holiday cottage. And if I can't, it's a cow shed.'

✻ ✻ ✻ • ✻ ✻ ✻ • ✻ ✻ ✻

An Irishman was doing his first parachute jump. At 30,000 feet his parachute wouldn't open. As he plummeted downwards, he saw another Irishman soaring upwards.

'Here,' he called, 'do you know anything about parachutes?'

'No,' said the other Irishman. 'Do you know anything about gas cookers?'

✻ ✻ ✻ • ✻ ✻ ✻ • ✻ ✻ ✻

An Irishman went into a pet shop to buy some birdseed. The shopkeeper handed over a packet.

'So how deep do I plant them, and how long will it be before I grow some birds?'

✻ ✻ ✻ • ✻

A man went into a Belfast fish and chip shop.

'Fish and chips twice, please.'
The woman behind the counter looked up from the frier.

'It's OK, I heard you the first time.'

An Irishman is concerned because his wife thinks she is a washing line.

'Very strange,' says the doctor. 'You'd best bring her in.'

'What!' exclaimed the Irishman. 'And have all my washing fall on the ground?'

Did you hear about the Irish builder who didn't know the difference between toothpaste and putty?
He slammed the door at home once and all his windows fell out!

Did you hear about the Irishman who decided to go on a hitch-hiking holiday?
He left early to avoid the traffic!

An Irishman was leaving a restaurant.

'Excuse me, waiter. Have you seen my hat?'

'It's on your head, Sir.'

'Don't bother then,' said the Irishman. 'I'll look for it myself.'

An Irishwoman went into her local baker's and asked for a loaf of bread.

'I'm afraid that bread has gone up another 10p today,' said the baker.

'Oh dear, has it?' said the Irishwoman.

'Well in that case give me one of yesterday's loaves.'

'Why don't you go out and find some work?' a fed up Irishwoman said to her idle husband.

'I can't; I'm frightened!' said her husband.

'Frightened of what?' asked the Irishwoman.

'Finding some.'

Did you hear about the Irishman who was really tight with money?

He sent his brother, who lived in Liverpool, a homing pigeon for his birthday!

A man was being trained by the Irish Parachute Team and was about to jump.

'What happens if my parachute doesn't open?'

'Bring it back and we'll replace it!' shouted the instructor.

'So Pat, how long did you work last week?'

'One day,' replied Pat.

His friend sighed.

'Oh it must be nice to have a steady job like that.'

Detective O'Malley arrived at the scene of the crime and approached the Irish policeman on duty.

'Was the victim seriously wounded?'

'Well, Sir, two of the injuries were fatal, but the third was just a flesh wound.'

An Irishwoman went shopping at the new supermarket.

'I'd like some pepper, please.'

'Certainly, Miss,' said the assistant. 'What sort; Ground, Seeds, Black or Cayenne?'

'Toilet.'

Whilst on holiday in Ireland, an Englishman has a slow puncture in one of his tyres, so he pulls in to a service station.

'I say my good man, what do you have in the shape of tyres?'

The Irishman behind the counter thinks for a moment.

'Doughnuts, pancakes, biscuits, CDs and a couple of kid's hoops in the toy section.'

Two Irishmen were sitting on a train.

'Does this train stop at Waterford?'

'It does,' said the other.

'When?' asked the first Irishman.

'Oh, just watch me,' said the other Irishman, 'and get off two stops before I do.'

※ ✳ ※ • ※ ✳ ※ • ※ ✳ ※

'Doc, you've got to help me!' said an Irishman. 'I snore so loud at night that I keep waking myself up. What do you suggest?'

'Have you tried sleeping in another room?'

'I have,' the Irishman sighed. 'But I can still hear myself.'

※ ✳ ※ • ※ ✳ ※ • ※ ✳ ※

Two Irish fashion designers were on holiday in Africa, and were walking past a river when they saw a crocodile swim past with a man's head in its mouth.

'Oh bejabers!' said one of the designers. 'Did you see that?'

'I did!' replied the second designer. 'I never knew that Lacoste did sleeping bags.'

No one was saying that Phil O'Food wasn't suited for his job in the restaurant kitchen, but on his first day the chef caught him trying to open an egg with a tin opener.

Two Irish kiddies were talking in the playground.
'My dad could beat up your dad!' said one.
'That's no big deal,' said the other. 'So can my mum!'

Did you hear about the pregnant Irishwoman who wanted to have her baby in the big supermarket?
She heard they did a free delivery service!

'Excuse me, do you serve women in this pub?' the Irishman asked the landlord.
'No we don't, Sir,' said the landlord. 'You have to bring your own.'

An Irishman went in to a hotel and saw a sign that said "Please ring the bell for the receptionist". He rang it, and the receptionist duly arrived.
'Now, why can't you ring that little bell yourself?' the Irishman asked.

Carrie Cash went into her local cheese shop.

'I'd like your strongest Irish cheese, please.'

The shopkeeper called out to the back of the shop.

'Are you there Margaret? Unchain number 26.'

Did you hear the one about the Irishman who was absolutely useless at cards?

Every time he was dealt a spade, he'd spit on his hands and rub them together!

'Have you seen my boots?' the Irishman asked his wife.

'No I haven't,' answered his wife. 'Are you sure you had them on when you took them off?'

An Irish girl went in to Boots and asked for a bar of soap.

'Would you like it scented?' asked the lady on the counter.

'No thanks,' said the girl. 'I'll take it with me.'

An American went to Dublin market. At a fruit and veg stall he picked up a melon.

'Hey Buddy,' he said sarcastically to the Irish stallholder, 'are these the biggest apples you do?'

'Here you, put that grape down!'

Did you hear the one about the Irishman who broke the world 100 metre record whilst wearing his walking boots?

He fell off a cliff!

An Irishman was taking his first ever trip on a train when the ticket collector approached him.

'Ticket please.'

'No way!' said the Irishman. 'I've paid for mine, you get your own.'

An Irishman was having his flying lesson when the instructor turned to him.

'You're doing so well, tomorrow you will fly solo.'

'How low is that then?' asked the Irishman.

Did you hear the one about the Irish motor mechanic who started drinking brake fluid? He drank so much of the stuff that his boss was worried that he was becoming addicted to it.

'I'm not addicted to it,' he told his boss. 'I can stop any time!'

A man was staying in a hotel in Dublin when he received a call from the reception desk.

'Excuse me, Sir,' said the soft Irish voice on the other end of the phone. 'This is Jilly on reception. Sorry to bother you, but what time did you want calling this morning? Was it seven o'clock or eight o'clock?'

'Er, what's the time now?' asked the man.

'Twenty to ten.'

❋ ❋ ❋ • ❋ ❋ ❋ • ❋ ❋ ❋

Why aren't Irishmen allowed to hold car-boot sales? They keep selling the engines of the cars that have been reversed in!

❋ ❋ ❋ • ❋ ❋ ❋ • ❋ ❋ ❋

Two priests are standing on the road holding up two signs that read: 'The End Is Near.' And 'Turn back before it's too late.'

A car approaches and the driver winds down his window and shouts.

'Get off the road and get back in church, yer eejits.'

The car screeches on past them and around the bend in the road. Suddenly there is a screech of tyres and a big splash. One priest says to the other:

'Do you think we should change the signs to just say BRIDGE OUT?'

A drunk Irishman was walking down a Dublin street shouting at everyone he passed.

'Sage! Parsley! Thyme!

Rosemary! Sage! Parsley!

Thyme! Rosemary!'

He was later arrested for 'Herbal Abuse'.

'What happened to you?' the Irishman's wife asked him when he arrived home soaking wet. 'Is it raining?'

'No it isn't,' he said, 'but that's the last time I take my motorbike through that car wash.'

An Irishman went horse riding the other week, but never again. It all started off fine. The Irishman got on the horse, held onto the reins, but then the horse started bouncing out of control. The Irishman tried to hang on, but the horse was bucking so much that he fell off. Unfortunately for the Irishman, his foot got caught in a stirrup and he hit his head on the ground as the horse refused to stop or slow down. Slowly, and with colossal effort, the Irishman managed to pull himself up by grabbing hold of the stirrup. He was almost back in the saddle when suddenly... the shop manager came and turned the ride off!

'So how're you getting on selling your old car?' Thaddy asked.

'Not very well,' said Paddy, 'on account of it having 195,000 miles on the clock.'

'Don't worry about that,' said Thaddy. 'I've got a mate who works in a garage who will turn the clock back to 50,000 miles for a couple of pounds.'

The following week Thaddy and Paddy met again.

'Did you take your car to my mate?'

'Yeah!' smiled Paddy.

'Did he put the mileage back?'

'He certainly did.' Paddy smiled even more.

'And have you sold the car now?' Thaddy enquired.

'No,' replied Paddy.

'Why not?' asked Thaddy.

'Didn't see the point. It only had 50,000 on the clock.'

~~~~~~~~~~~~~~~~~~~~~

'Doctor. I'm really worried about my brother,' the Irish girl said. 'He thinks he's an apple.'

'Oh dear,' said the doctor. 'I think I'd best have a look at him. Is he with you today?'

'Yes,' said the Irish girl.

'Is he in the waiting room?' asked the doctor.

'No,' said the Irish girl. 'He's in my pocket.'

An Irish boy bought his girlfriend her first mobile phone for her birthday. The next day she was out shopping and her phone rang. It was the Irish boy.

'Hi dear. How do you like your new phone?'

'It's wonderful,' said the Irish girl. 'But there's just one thing I don't understand?'

'What's that sweetheart?' asked the Irish boy.

'How did you know I would be here?'

❋ ❋ ❋ • ❋ ❋ ❋ • ❋ ❋ ❋

An Irishman had got a ticket to the Ireland rugby match, but when he got to the packed ground he found he was right at the back of the stand. He looked around and there, right at the front of the terrace was another Irishman sitting next to an empty chair. The Irishman jostled his way to the front and asked the man if he could sit in the empty chair.

'Sure,' said his fellow Irishman. 'It was my wife's seat. We always used to watch this fixture, year after year, but she passed away, shortly after I bought the tickets.'

'Oh I'm sorry,' said the Irishman, 'but couldn't you have given the ticket to a friend or a relative, so you wouldn't be alone?'

'Not today,' sighed the other Irishman. 'They're all at her funeral.'

Pat comes rushing home from school one day.

'Mammy, we learnt to count at school today. All the other boys only counted to 5, but I counted to 10.'

'Well done!' said Pat's mammy.

'Is that because I'm Irish, Mammy?' he beamed.

'Yes darling, it is because you're Irish.'

'Another thing we did today was the alphabet. All the other boys only got to D, but I got to L.'

'Excellent!' said Pat's mammy.

'Is that because I'm Irish, Mammy?' he beamed.

'Yes darling, it is because you're Irish.'

'Oh and when we went swimming, mammy, I had a hairy chest, but the other boys didn't. Is that because I'm Irish, Mammy?'

'No darling,' said Pat's mammy. 'It's because you're 26.'

❋ ❋ ❋ • ❋ ❋ ❋ • ❋ ❋ ❋

'Is your car OK now?' asked Mary as she and Colleen met up in local Charles Dickens-themed wine bar 'Grape Expectations'.

'Yes, thank goodness!' said Colleen. 'To be honest I thought the mechanic would try and rip me off because I was a blonde Irishwoman.'

'And did he?'

'No he didn't!' beamed Colleen. 'I was so relieved when he only charged me £40 for new indicator fluid.'

Did you hear about the Irishman who complained to the Irish TV network about all the sex, nudity, foul language and violence on television?
It was actually the tape on his video recorder!

An Irishman was in hospital awaiting a brain operation, but wanted a word with the surgeon.

'What seems to be the problem?'

'Well, I've just been speaking to the English guy in the next bed,' said the Irishman. 'He's having the same operation as me, and it's costing him £1000 less than mine. So what I want to know is why you charge me more?'

'You're Irish,' said the Surgeon.

'What's that got to do with it?' asked the Irishman.

'We always charge a search fee.'

An Irishman goes into a bar and orders 9 pints of stout. To the amazement of the barman he drinks them down one after the other.

'Ah that was great,' says the Irishman wiping his mouth. 'But I shouldn't have done that with what I've got.'

'Why, what have you got?' asked the barman.

'About a pound.'

An elderly Irish couple are on holiday in Wales when they come across and road sign that read "Llanfairp-wllgwyngyllgogerychwyrndrobwllllantysiliogogogoch"

Both try to pronounce it, but end up arguing. They are still arguing when they go into a restaurant in the town for lunch. The waiter appears to take their order.

'We're from Ireland and we were just wondering how you pronounce where we are?'

'And could you do it slowly?' adds the wife.

The waiter shrugs his shoulders.

'Liiiiiiitttttttllllleeee Chhhheeeeeeffffffff!'

~~~~~~~~~~~~~~~~~~~~~~

The manager of the Kilkenny Social Club is woken up by a 3am phone call.

'What time does the club open?' the voice slurred.

'Midday!' said the manager and hung up.

An hour later the phone rang again – it was the same person.

'What time does the club open?'

'Like I said earlier!' snapped the manager. 'Midday.' Again she slammed the phone down. At 5:30am the phone rang again and the mumbling voice sounded even more drunk.

'Excuse me Miss, but what time did you say that the club opened?'

'Look I've already told you twice: Midday,' The manager shouted angrily down the line. 'And if you don't sober up, you won't be allowed in.'

'In?' said the voice. 'I don't want to get in, I want to get out.'

The Irishman asked his dying mother if she would like to be buried or cremated.

'Oh I don't know, son,' said his mother. 'Surprise me!'

❋ ＊ ❋ ● ❋ ＊ ❋ ● ❋ ＊ ❋

An Irishman was the first human ever to undergo a tortoise heart transplant. The operation was a complete success, and he was able to leave hospital a month later. Three weeks after that, he reached the car park!

❋ ＊ ❋ ● ❋ ＊ ❋ ● ❋ ＊ ❋

Did you hear the one about the dyslexic Irish twins? Every full moon one changed into a warehouse, and his brother became an atheist who didn't believe in dog!

❋ ＊ ❋ ● ❋ ＊ ❋ ● ❋ ＊ ❋

Paddy and Pat had gone out hunting, but got lost as it started to get dark. Paddy mentioned that he read somewhere that the best thing to do was to stay in one place, fire three shots and wait for someone to find you. So that's what they did.

Two hours passed and still nobody had come.

So Paddy suggested that they fire another three shots into the night sky and wait.

Three hours passed and still nothing.

'Fire three more shots,' said Paddy.

'OK,' said Pat, 'but I hope someone comes soon – we're running out of arrows.'

There was a knock on an Irishman's door one morning. When he opened it, a very angry neighbour confronted him.

'I left my house to go for a newspaper and that dog of yours went for me!' he snapped.

'Well would you believe it?' said the Irishman. 'I've had that dog for ten years. I've fed it, looked after it, walked it and in all that time it's never once got the paper for me.'

✳ ✳ ✳ • ✳ ✳ ✳ • ✳ ✳ ✳

Liam and Shaun were sitting in a pub. The wall opposite them had a very large mirror on it.

'Here Shaun,' said Liam. 'Don't look now, but there are a couple of fellas over there the spitting image of you and me.'

Shaun looked over and was astonished.

'So they are. Same clothes, same hair. That's amazing!'

'I tell you what,' said Liam standing up. 'I'm going to buy them a drink.'

'No sit down, Liam,' whispered Shaun. 'The one that looks like you is coming over.'

Paddy's mammy rang him at home one evening.

'Paddy, your sister has had a baby!' she said excitedly.

'Oh that's great, Mammy,' replied Paddy.

'I haven't found out yet, if it's a boy or a girl,' his mammy told him, 'so I can't tell you if you're an uncle or aunt.'

A TV documentary had shown a couple of anglers in Scotland catching salmon, one holding the legs of the other while he dangled over a bridge, catching fish as they swam up river. Thinking this an excellent idea, Liam and Shaun decided to try it themselves.

They found a bridge. Liam dangled Shaun over. About half an hour passed.

'Liam, Liam, pull me up quick!'

'Have you caught a salmon, Shaun?' Liam asked excitedly.

'Not yet. There's a train coming.'

Paddy O'Pudding, Ireland's fattest man, fell into the crocodile enclosure at Dublin Zoo. The keepers did all they could, but by the time they hoisted him out, he had eaten three crocodiles.

'I'm not going to my local hospital any more!' the Irishman said.

'Why not?' asked his wife.

'Well I went there today and there was a sign on the door: "Guide Dogs operating here." I know they're clever and everything, but there's got to be a limit.'

'Mammy, I think you might be colour blind,' said the little Irish girl as she started to eat her dessert.

'I don't think so,' said her Mammy. 'What makes you say that?'

'This rhubarb tart has got celery in it.'

The Irish mathematics teacher stood up in front of the class.

'There are three types of people in this world: those who can count and those who can't.'

An Irishman went for a job as a tree feller and on his first day chopped down an amazing 200 trees. The foreman was very, very impressed.

'Hey, that's fantastic work. Where did you learn to cut down trees like that?'

'In the Sahara Forest,' replied the Irishman.

'Surely you mean the Sahara Desert?' said the Foreman.

'Well, that's what they call it now.'

Barry and Carrie were getting married. The guests were going into the church and the ushers were showing them to their seats.

Would you be a friend of the groom?' asked the chief usher.

'Certainly not!' snapped the lady. 'I'm the mother of the bride.'

※ ＊ ※ ● ＊ ＊ ※ ● ※ ＊ ※

An Irish girl was crying at her work desk. Her boss asked what was wrong.

'I got a phone call this morning from my Da saying that my Mammy has died.'

'Oh I'm so sorry. Look why don't you take the day off?'

'No thank you,' sniffed the Irish girl. 'Being here helps me to take my mind off things for a while.'

'Are you sure?'

'Yes, thank you, I'll be fine now I've had a good cry.'

Hoping she was OK the boss returned to his office. Ten minutes later he was told that the Irish girl is sobbing her heart out again.

'What's the matter?' he asked.

'Oh it's awful, I can't take much more,' the Irish girl sobbed.

'What is it?' The boss asked anxiously.

'My sister has just rung and... and... her Mammy has just died too,' the Irish girl wailed.

An Irish girl went for a job interview and the interviewer asked her age.

'Let me see,' she said, as she started counting on her fingers, then slipped off her shoes and counted her toes. '19.'

'OK,' said the interviewer. 'And how tall are you?' The girl reached into her handbag, took out a tape measure and measured herself. 'I'm 5ft 3 inches tall,' she smiled.

'What's your name?'

'Oh, I know this one! Just hang on a minute, it'll come to me. Now let's see…

Happy Birthday to me, Happy Birthday to me, Happy Birthday dear… Mary!'

✳ ✳ ✳ • ✳ ✳ ✳ • ✳ ✳ ✳

'I hope you don't mind me asking but what's that on the side of your face?' an Irishman asked a man he had just met.

'Not at all,' replied the man. 'It's a birthmark.'

'Oh I see!' said the Irishman. 'And how long have you had that then?'

An Irishman was sitting in front of an old Irish biddy on a long coach journey. During the ride she tapped him on the shoulder and offered him a handful of peanuts, which he accepted, as he was hungry. About 15 minutes later she did the same, tapped the Irishman on the shoulder and gave him some peanuts. She did this a number of times throughout the trip. When the coach reached its final destination and the old biddy had given the Irishman her last handful of peanuts, he was curious.

'Why did you keep giving me all those peanuts?'

'Well because with my old teeth, I can't eat them,' she grinned.

'Why did you buy them, then?' asked the Irishman.

'Because I like licking off the chocolate coating.'

~~~~~~~~~~~~~~~~~~~~

Two Irishmen were playing golf. They were on the eighteenth hole and one was taking a very long time before he played the shot.

'Come on. What you playing at?' said his friend.

'I want this to be my best shot ever. My wife is watching me from the clubhouse steps.'

'Oh don't be stupid,' said his friend. 'You'll never hit her from here.'

~~~~~~~~~~~~~~~~~~~~

Did you hear the one about the Irishman who called 3am in the morning 'A pig's tail'?
Well, it was twirly!

An Irishman went to Las Vegas and tried his luck on the roulette table. He placed his first bet on number 7 and lost. He put more money on number 7, and lost again. Next time round, he chose number 7, placed his bet and lost. Finally, with only a few dollars left, he was about to place a final bet on number 7 when another gambler said:

'Why don't you try a different number?'

'Are you joking?' said the Irishman. 'Seven is my lucky number!'

Dolan was always late for work because he overslept. His boss warned him that if he didn't do something about it, he would be fired. So Dolan went to his doctor who gave him a pill to take just before he went to bed. Dolan slept really well and was up before the alarm went off. He was up so early that he had time to have breakfast and walk to work. He was even at his desk before his boss arrived.

'Morning boss!' Dolan grinned and told him all about the pill.

'That's all very well, Dolan,' said his boss. 'But where were you yesterday?'

An Irishman was very worried about the truck he was driving behind and tried desperately to get the driver to stop. Finally the truck came to some traffic lights and stopped. An Irishman jumped out and in a panic rushed up to the driver's door.

'What's the matter?' asked the driver.

'I tried to stop you earlier!' the Irishman said urgently. 'It's your load; you're losing it. It's going all over the road.'

The driver gave a look.

'I drive a gritter.'

A blind Irishman and his guide dog walk into a shop. He stops, picks up his dog by its lead and starts swinging it around his head.

'Excuse me, Sir,' says a concerned shop assistant. 'Can I help you?'

'No thanks,' said the blind Irishman. 'I'm just having a look around.'

An Irishman wanted to start his own zoo so he wrote to his local pet store. He wasn't sure if he was using the correct collective noun when he asked for two mongooses. He tried two "mongi", but that didn't sound right; and he tried "mongeeses" and that didn't sound any better. In the end he wrote this letter:

'Dear Sir,

I am starting my own zoo. Please can you send me a mongoose?

PS: And can you send me another one as well?'

The young Irishwoman was distraught when the policeman turned up after she had called to say that her car had been broken into.

'I don't believe it!' she wailed. 'They've taken the CD player, the radio, the steering wheel, the glove compartment, the dash board, the gear stick...'

'Madam, let's calm down,' said the policeman. 'Would you like to get out of the back seat?'

✳ ✳ ✳ • ✳ ✳ ✳ • ✳ ✳ ✳

Farmer O'Dell and Farmer O'Dingle were driving their tractor down the middle of a narrow country road. Suddenly a car comes around the corner: the driver sees the tractor and slams on the brakes to avoid it. The car skids, hits an embankment, flips over a couple of times and lands in a field where the driver crawls out through the window.

'That's lucky,' said Farmer O'Dell. 'A couple of minutes earlier and we would still be in that field.'

✳ ✳ ✳ • ✳

Why are Irish jokes so simple?
So that everybody else in the world can understand them!

It was 2am when Bob's wife woke him up, telling him that someone was knocking on the front door. Bob got up, trudged downstairs and opened the door. Standing on the doorstep was a drunk Irishman.

'Sorry to disturb you Sir, so I am, but do you think you could give me a push?'

'Do you know what time it is?' snapped Bob. 'Go away.' He slammed the door and went back to bed.

'Oh that wasn't very nice,' said his wife when he told her. 'Remember that time we were on holiday in Ireland and our car broke down? That kind Irishman gave us a push.'

'OK, OK,' said Bob as he went back downstairs and opened the door. He couldn't see anyone, but called out.

'Do you still want a push?'

'Yes please,' slurred an Irish voice.

'Where are you?' Bob called again.

'Over here!' called the drunken Irishman. 'On the swing.'

~~~~~~~~~~~~~~~~

'Well I know that!' shouted the Irish office worker. 'What do you think I am? An eejit?' She slammed down the phone just as her boss walked past.

'Is there a problem?' he asked.

'Not really,' she replied. 'Just some bozo telling me it's a long distance from Australia.'

'How much are your chickens?' a customer asked Farmer O'Dell.

'They're £7,' said the Farmer.

'And did you raise them yourself?'

'Oh yes,' said Farmer O'Dell. 'Yesterday they were £6.'

Liam was telling Shaun how he played Scrabble with his pet dog.

'Wow!' said Shaun. 'That's one clever dog.'

'Not really,' replied Liam. 'I've beaten him a couple of times and his spelling isn't that good.'

An Irish girl was on holiday. She was lying on her front while sunbathing, when a little boy walked past. He accidentally dropped his ice cream on her back. She screamed.

'Bejabers, those seagulls must live in a freezer.'

Three long time friends, an Englishman, a Scotsman and an Irishman were stranded on Desert Island when they found a Genie in a bottle. The Genie told the men that they could have one wish each.

'I wish I was playing for England in the World Cup final, just about to score the winning goal.'

The Genie clapped his hands, and there was the Englishman just about to receive a perfect cross from David Beckham. Back on the island the Scotsman was next.

'I wish I was playing for Scotland in the World Rugby cup final and I was just about to score the winning try against the Australians.'

The Genie clapped his hands, and there was the Scotsman running with the ball under his arm towards the line.

'OK, your turn!' the Genie said to the Irishman. 'What do you want?'

The Irishman thought for a while.

'Well now everyone's gone, I'm really lonely. I wish my friends were with me.'

❈ ✳ ❈ • ❈ ✳ ❈ • ❈ ✳ ❈

A tourist was talking to an Irishman in a pub one day.

'Why do you Irish people talk in questions?'

The Irishman thought for a while.

'Do we? Is that so? Well, whoever would have guessed?'

An Irishman had promised his wife he would give up the drink, although he had been drinking heavily in the pub and it was now time to go home.

He stood up to go and promptly fell to the floor. Picking himself up and using chairs and tables, he wobbled to the door of the pub, opened it and fell into the street. No matter how much he tried, every time he managed to stand up, he fell flat on his face.

Eventually the Irishman crawled home, managing to open his front door before he fell into his house. He crawled up the stairs and into his bedroom where his wife was sleeping. With one last effort the Irishman stood up, wobbled then fell onto the bed and into a deep sleep.

When he woke next morning his wife was standing over him.

'You've been drinking, haven't you?'

'What makes you think that, dearest?' asked the bleary-eyed Irishman.

'Because the pub's just phoned to say that you left your crutches there again last night!'

'Here, I've given up betting,' said the Irishman.

'Bet you haven't.'

'Bet you, I have.'

'How much?'

'Ten pounds?'

~~~~~~~~~~~~~~~~

Paddy was busy digging a hole on a Dublin building site when his foreman came up and asked if he would like to buy a raffle ticket.

'What for?' asked Paddy.

'You know the crane driver suddenly died of a heart attack last week?'

'Yes,' said Paddy.

'Well it's for his wife and five kids.'

'Oh, no thanks then,' replied Paddy. 'I've already got a wife and kids and I don't want to win any more.'

~~~~~~~~~~~~~~~~

An Irishman was talking to another about an article in the paper.

'It said that one in five people in the world are Chinese and there are five people in my family.'

'So?' said his friend.

'Well that means one of them must be Chinese. I know it's not me, so it's either me Mam and Da or me little sister Mary, or me older brother Ho-Chin-Lou. So I reckon it must be Mary.'

'Well,' said the doctor to the Irishman. 'I've given you a thorough examination and I think you should give up the stout, the women, the gambling and the singing.'

'Oh I see,' says the concerned Irishman. 'Will that help me live longer?'

'Well,' the doctor replied, 'it will certainly feel like it.'

~~~~~~~~~~~~~~~~~

'What happened?' an Irishman asked his neighbour when he saw him on crutches with his leg in plaster.

'I broke it playing table tennis,' said his neighbour.

'Playing table tennis?' the Irishman laughed. 'How did you manage that?'

'Well, I won and tried to jump the net.'

~~~~~~~~~~~~~~~~~

An Irishman went into a restaurant and ordered lobster. When it arrived, he wasn't happy and called over the waiter.

'This lobster has only got one claw!' he complained.

'I know Sir,' sniffed the waiter. 'He lost it in a fight.'

'Well take this one back,' snapped the Irishman, 'and bring me the winner.'

Old Mrs Kelly answered the door to a man who asked after her husband.

'Is Mr Kelly in?'

'I'm afraid he's dead,' said old Mrs Kelly.

'Oh I'm so sorry to hear that,' replied the man. 'When did he die?'

'Well,' began old Mrs Kelly, 'if he had lived 'til tomorrow, he'd have been dead for a fortnight.'

✱ ✱ ✱ • ✱ ✱ ✱ • ✱ ✱ ✱

A woman goes into a shop and asks for an Irish sausage.

'Are you Irish?' asked the shop assistant.

'I am, but I don't see what that has to do with it. If I asked for a German sausage, would you ask me if I was German? If I asked for an Italian sausage would you assume I was Italian?'

'Well, no,' said the shop assistant.

'So why, when I ask for an Irish sausage, do you ask me if I'm Irish?'

'Because this is a book shop!'

✱ ✱ ✱ • ✱ ✱ ✱ • ✱ ✱ ✱

There was a fatal accident at the Dublin Distillery last week. Pat O'Butter fell into a giant vat of Irish whiskey. His work colleagues tried to save him, but he fought them off bravely.

He drowned, eventually, after getting out three times to go to the toilet.

After his funeral he was cremated, and it took four days to put the fire out.

Two Irish mothers were talking, when the first told the second that she had ten children, all boys.

'Ten!' said the other mother. 'What's their names?'

'Patrick, Patrick, Patrick, Patrick, Patrick, Patrick, Patrick, Patrick, Patrick and Patrick.'

'Why did you give them all the same name?' asked the second mother.

'To make life simple!' said the first mother. 'If I want them to come in from playing I just shout "Patrick"; and they all come. If I want them to come to dinner I just shout "Patrick" and they all come.'

'But what if you only want one of them?' said the second woman.

'Oh that's when it gets a bit difficult; then I have to use their surname as well.'

❋ ❋ ❋ ● ❋ ❋ ❋ ● ❋ ❋ ❋

An Irish workman walks into a pub with a rolled up strip of tarmac under his arm.

'Pint of the black stuff, please, and one for the road.'

❋ ❋ ❋ ● ❋

'Daddy, I'm going to ask Father Christmas for "Divorced Barbie",' said the little Irish girl.

'Why?' asked her dad.

'Because with "Divorced Barbie" you not only get all her clothes, but you get all Ken's clothes, Ken's car, Ken's boat and Ken's House.'

'I've finally found out that me and the wife have something in common,' an Irishman told his friend.

'And what's that?'

'We were married on the same day.'

~~~~~~~~~~~~~~~~~

'Have you seen these new Irish Whiskey bottles?' Liam asked Shaun.

'No,' said Shaun. 'What's different about them?'

'Well they've got instructions on the bottom and top of the bottle. On the bottom of this one it says "Open other end".'

'And what does it say on the top?' asked Shaun.

'"See other end for instructions".'

~~~~~~~~~~~~~~~~~

An Irishman had nearly completed his driving test. The driving instructor was asking him some road sign questions.

'OK. What does an unbroken single yellow line mean?'

'No parking at all,' said the Irishman.

'Well done! Now what does two unbroken yellow lines mean?'

The Irishman thought for a while.

'No parking at all, at all.'

Three old Irish biddies, Mary, Martha and Marie, were sitting in Mary's kitchen talking about getting old.

'It's getting terrible,' says Mary. 'I go to the cupboard with a pot of jam and I can't remember if I'm putting it away or making a sandwich!'

'Me too,' adds Martha. 'I sometimes find myself half way up the stairs, wondering if I'm going up or down.'

'Well I must be lucky,' says Marie. 'I don't suffer from those sort of problems, touch wood.' She taps the table. 'Did you hear that? Someone must be at the door, I'll just go and get it.'

It was an Irish girl's first time on a plane. No sooner had she sat in a nice window seat than a man came up to her and said that she was sitting in his seat.

'I'm not!' protested the Irish girl.

'You are,' repeated the man.

'Well I don't think I am!' snapped the Irish girl. 'I'm not for moving.'

The man held up his hands and sighed. 'OK, OK, you sit there, but you'll have to fly the plane.'

The Irishman finally came to bed at 3 in the morning. His wife asked him why he had stayed up so late.

'It's the cat's fault!' he said.

'Why?' asked his wife.

'I was waiting for him to come in,' yawned the Irishman, 'so I could put him out for the night.'

✳ ✳ ✳ • ✳ ✳ ✳ • ✳ ✳ ✳

An Irishman was talking to an American in a Dublin bar about his forthcoming summer holiday to the States.

'So where are you staying?'

'I'm thinking of San Josay,' said the Irishman.
The American laughed. 'That's pronounced San Hosay. In California we pronounce 'J' as 'H'.'

'Oh thanks,' said the Irishman. 'I didn't know that.'

'No problem. So when are you going?'

'Hune and Huly,' replied the Irishman.

✳ ✳ ✳ • ✳ ✳ ✳ • ✳ ✳ ✳

Pat was walking past Paddy's house when he saw a sign that read 'Boat for Sale'. Paddy was in the garden at the time.

'What's this sign all about Paddy? You haven't got a boat – all you've got out here is a old lawnmower and a garden bench!'

'I know,' said Paddy, 'and they're boat for sale.'

A drunk wobbles into the pub and sees another man sitting at the bar.

'Can I buy you a drink?' says the drunk.

'Sure, that'll be great,' the man replies in an Irish accent.

'Hey, are you from Ireland?' asks the drunk as he gives the man his drink.

'And proud of it,' the man smiles.

The drunk responds. 'I'm from Ireland too! Let's have another drink for Ireland.' So they have another round.

'So what part of Ireland are you from?'

'County Mayo.'

'No?!' exclaims the drunk. 'I'm from County Mayo too.'

'Let's drink to County Mayo,' says the Irishman.

'What school did you go to?' slurred the drunk.

'St Mary's. I left in 1977.'

The drunk sputtered into his beer. 'I went to St Mary's and I left in 1977!'

'Another round please, barman.'

As the barman pulled their next round a regular came into the pub. 'What's happening?'

'Not much,' sighed the barman, 'apart from the Flynn twins getting drunk again.'

'Haven't seen you in here for a while,' Paddy said to Thaddy when he turned up for a drink in his local pub.

'I know,' said Thaddy. 'I've had to stay at home with the missus because of the abusive phone calls.'

'Oh I'm sorry mate. It's not nice when that happens,' sympathised Paddy.

'It's OK now. She's promised not to make any more.'

~~~~~~~~~~~~~~~~~~~~~~~~~~~~

Dolan was a fanatical supporter of Ireland's worst football team, Shamrock United Rovers Athletic. At one match a man next to him started talking to him.

'Are you going to stay to the end?'

'Of course!' said Dolan.

'Here's the keys then. Lock up on your way out.'

~~~~~~~~~~~~~~~~~~~~~~~~~~~~

An Irishman has a great party trick. He holds up his two thumbs and gets someone to choose one. When they have, he puts both his hands behind his back for a moment and then holds out his clenched fists.

'OK, which hand?'

Shamus was puzzled by an interesting article in the newspaper.

'Paddy, it says here that 8 of 10 men use ball point pens to write with.'

'So?' said Paddy.

'Well,' asked a curious Shamus, 'what do the other two use them for?'

How can you tell if you've brought an Irish ladder?
It has a sign at the top that reads 'Stop'!

A driver ran into a small train station outside Cork looking for the station-master.

'Excuse me,' he gasped, 'it's your level crossing. One of the barriers is up and the other one is down. Is everything OK?'

'Ah now, don't be worrying yourself,' said the station-master, 'we're half expecting a train.'

Paddy was telling Pat about a disturbing sight from the previous night.

'Oh it was horrible, Pat,' Paddy said. 'It had 32 legs, 32 arms, 12 teeth and was all wrinkled and smelled like a vapour rub.'

'Bejabers Paddy, what was it? Some kind of monster?'

'No,' replied Pat. 'The front row of a Val Doonican tribute concert.'

A young Irish lad was talking to his fiancée.

'I want to marry an intelligent woman, a good woman, and a woman who will make me happy.'

'Will you please make up your mind?'

* * * • * * * • * * *

An Irish girl rang the doctor in a panic one morning.

'Doctor, I've just woken up and I've got a pimple on the side of my face.'

'So?' replied the doctor. 'Most people have pimples on the side of their faces at some time.'

'But this one has a tiny tree growing from it!' said the Irish girl. 'And under the tree is a little pond and next to that is a tiny set of chairs and a table with a picnic laid out on it.'

'Oh there's nothing to worry about,' said the doctor. 'It's just a beauty spot.'

* * * • * * * • * * *

A man went into a Dublin bank and asked the cashier if she could check his balance.

'Certainly, Sir,' said the Irish cashier. She got up, walked around to the man's side of the counter and pushed him over.

* * * • * * * • * * *

An American and an Irish tourist were looking at the Niagara Falls.

'Will you look at that. What a sight! I bet you don't have anything like that in Ireland?'

'We don't,' said the Irishman. 'But we've got plumbers who could fix it.'

Two Irish girls were discussing what to get their friend for her birthday.

'What about a book?' suggested one of them.

'No,' said her friend. 'She's already got one of those and she hasn't coloured it in yet!'

Imagine the Christmas story if the Three Wise Men had been Three Irish Mothers.
They wouldn't have had to ask for directions, they would have arrived on time, helped deliver the baby, cleaned up the stable, made a nice Irish stew and brought practical presents.

'I helped my husband become a millionaire,' the Irish girl boasted.

'Really,' said her friend. 'And what was he before?'

'A billionaire,' sighed the Irish girl.

An ageing Irish playboy sidles up to a pretty young girl at a party.

'I say gorgeous, where have you been all my life?'
The young girl looked at him, disgusted.

'Well, for most of it, I wasn't born.'

Two Irish tramps were paddling in the sea when one of them looked down at the other's feet.

'Bejabers. Your feet are filthy.'

'I know,' said the second Irish tramp. 'We didn't come here last year.'

~~~~~~~~~~~~~~~~~~~~~~~~~~~~~~~~

An Irishman went for a job. The interviewer asked him his name.

'Oh now, that's a difficult one. I've to think about that one.'

'Concentrate,' said the interviewer.

'No, it's longer than that!' replied the Irishman.

~~~~~~~~~~~~~~~~~~~~~~~~~~~~~~~~

Now I'm not saying that Titch O'Malley was the smallest man in Ireland, but he was late for work the other day because he was cleaning out the budgie's cage and the door slammed shut.

~~~~~~~~~~~~~~~~~~~~~~~~~~~~~~~~

An Irishman was hitchhiking along a road when a big black hearse stopped beside him.

The driver offered him a lift.

'No thanks,' said the Irishman. 'I wasn't thinking of going that far!'

The Wicklow fire brigade had just received a brand new fire engine.

'So what are we going to do with the old engine?' asked one of the fire fighters. 'Are we going to dump it?'

'No we're not,' said the Station chief. 'We'll use the old one for false alarms.'

You don't see too many Irish snowmen around, do you?
That's because they take longer to build – you have to spend time hollowing the head out!

Did you hear the one about the Irish wife who showed her husband a picture of a very expensive outfit in a catalogue?
She told him that she would really like it, so the Irish husband cut it out and gave it to her!

'I'm sorry,' said the doctor. 'There's not a lot I can do for you. You are suffering from alcoholic constipation.'

'What do you mean, doc?' asked the Irishman. 'Is that serious?'

'You find it almost impossible to pass a pub.'

A young lad went into a joke shop in Dublin and asked the owner for some invisible ink.

'Certainly!' said the owner. 'What colour?'

Did you hear the one about the Irishwoman who flew all the way to Alaska to make her dinner?
She bought a ready meal whose instructions read, 'Prepare from a frozen state'!

Did you hear the one about the Irish inventor who crossed an electric blanket with a toaster?
It worked really well but he kept popping out of bed at night!

Did you hear the one about the Irish lighthouse keeper who bought a corner unit?
When he got it home he couldn't find anywhere to put it!

Paddy O'Paddy died and as he was a sailor all his life, requested that he be buried at sea. Unfortunately three Irish gravediggers died digging his grave.

Did you hear the one about the Irishwoman who went out with her purse open?
She heard on the radio that there was a chance of some change in the weather!

An Irishman went into his local library and slammed a book down on the counter.

'This book I borrowed last week was absolute rubbish. It had far too many characters, very little in the way of dialogue and absolutely no plot whatsoever.'

'Is that right?' said the Librarian. 'So you were the person who took our phone book!'

❋ ❋ ❋ • ❋ ❋ ❋ • ❋ ❋ ❋

Did you hear the one about the Irishwoman who would buy anything that was marked down?
She went out the other Saturday and bought three dresses and an escalator!

❋ ❋ ❋ • ❋ ❋ ❋ • ❋ ❋ ❋

Scientists in Germany have crossed a popular festive bird with an Irishman and got a turkey that looks forward to Christmas.

❋ ❋ ❋ • ❋

Did you hear about the young Irish girl who was disappointed when she watched *Pop Idol*?
She was expecting a show about lazy dads!

It was an Irishman's first day on a Dublin building site and he climbed up a very tall ladder, but when he got to the top he felt very dizzy.

'Oh I don't feel too well!' he called down to the foreman.

'Well come on down then,' said the foreman.

'How will I get down?' asked the Irishman.

'The same way you got up.'

'Oh I won't be doing that,' said the Irishman.

'Why not?' shouted the foreman.

'I came up head first.'

~~~~~~~~~~~~~~~~

An Englishman, a Scotsman and an Irishman were stopped on High Street by the police and asked for their names. Not wishing to give their real names the Englishman looked about and then said 'John Sainsburys.' The Scotsman looked around and said 'Mark Spencer.' The Irishman did the same and said 'Bradford and Bingley Building Society.'

~~~~~~~~~~~~~~~~

Pat and Paddy were lying in bed together. Pat looked at Paddy and Paddy looked at Pat and Pat said, 'I don't think much of this wife swapping, do you?'

~~~~~~~~~~~~~~~~

Did you hear the one about the Irishman who bought himself a new set of skis?

Unfortunately he was very badly injured when he tried to slalom down a waterfall!

'Have you heard my new knock-knock joke?' asked Paddy.

'No I haven't,' answers Thaddy.

'Great,' says Paddy. 'You start.'

Did you hear the one about the Irishman who won the Dublin Marathon in record time?

He was asked to do a lap of honour!

An Irishman walks into a bar sporting a big black eye.

'Who gave you that?' asked the barman.

'Nobody gave it to me,' said the Irishman. 'I had to fight for it.'

Did you hear the one about Ireland's smallest builder?

His first ever job was on a building site for Lego!

An Irishman was dead against fox hunting so he decided to be a hunt saboteur. He found out when the next local hunt was, went out the night before and shot the fox.

Did you hear the tale of the poor unfortunate Irishwoman who fell out of her window?

She was trying to iron her curtains!

'So, Paddy, my friend, how long have you believed in reincarnation?' Thaddy asked Paddy.

'Ever since I was a little frog.'

✳ ✳ ✳ ● ✳ ✳ ✳ ● ✳ ✳ ✳

Two Irish cannibals are eating a clown. One says to the other:

'Does this taste funny to you?'

✳ ✳ ✳ ● ✳ ✳ ✳ ● ✳ ✳ ✳

Three Irishmen went ice fishing but didn't catch a thing. By the time they cut a hole big enough for their boat, it was time to go home.

✳ ✳ ✳ ● ✳ ✳ ✳ ● ✳ ✳ ✳

How do you make an Irish person laugh on a Sunday?

Tell them a joke on a Friday night!

✳ ✳ ✳ ● ✳ ✳ ✳ ● ✳ ✳ ✳

The boss looked over the shoulder of his new Irish secretary.

'Your typing has really improved. I can only see five mistakes. Well done! Now type the second word.'

✳ ✳ ✳ ● ✳ ✳ ✳ ● ✳ ✳ ✳

An American tourist was visiting Ireland when he stopped outside O'Toole's farm for a chat.

'Nice farm, buddy,' he says. 'I got one at home in Texas. It takes me nearly six hours to drive all around it.'

'Is that right Sir? I've got a tractor like that too.'

An Irishman rang up his nearest cinema.

'Is that the local cinema?'

'Well now, that would depend on where you're calling from.'

✳ ✳ ✳ • ✳ ✳ ✳ • ✳ ✳ ✳

An Irishman wasn't feeling very well so he went to see his doctor, Dr Will C. U. Nye, for a check up. After some tests the doctor returned with the results and by the look on his face, it wasn't good news.

'I'm afraid I have some very bad news,' says the doctor. 'You are dying and you don't have long to live.'

Naturally the Irishman was distraught. 'Oh Doctor, how long have I got left?'

'Ten...' the doctor replies in a somewhat solemn tone.

'Ten?' cries the Irishman. 'Ten what? Years? Months? How long have I got left?'

The doctor answers, 'Nine, eight, seven...'

✳ ✳ ✳ • ✳

An Irishwoman found her husband standing in front of a mirror with his eyes closed.

'What you doing?' asked the Irishwoman.0

'Trying to see what I look like asleep,' said the Irishman.

Did you hear about the Irishman who went to a mind reader?
She gave him his money back after 30 seconds!

'Dad, can you help me with my homework?' the young Irish boy asked one night after school.

'Not really,' said his dad. 'It wouldn't be right.'

'I know Dad, but at least give it a try.'